KIM DIEHL

Simple Whatnots III

A THIRD SERVING OF SATISFYINGLY SCRAPPY QUILTS

C&T PUBLISHING
Another Maker Inspired!

Copyright © 2022 by Kim Diehl

Publisher: Amy Barrett-Daffin

Creative Director: Gailen Runge

Senior Editor: Roxane Cerda

Technical Editor: Nancy Mahoney

Cover And Interior Designer: Adrienne Smitke

Copy Editor: Sheila Chapman Ryan

Illustrator: Sandy Loi

Photographers: Adam Albright, and Brent Kane

Production Coordinator: Zinnia Heinzmann

Published by C&T Publishing, Inc., P.O. Box 1456, Lafayette, CA 94549

Attention Teachers: C&T Publishing, Inc., encourages the use of our books as texts for teaching. You can find lesson plans for many of our titles at ctpub.com or contact us at ctinfo@ctpub.com.

We take great care to ensure that the information included in our products is accurate and presented in good faith, but no warranty is provided, nor are results guaranteed. Having no control over the choices of materials or procedures used, neither the author nor C&T Publishing, Inc., shall have any liability to any person or entity with respect to any loss or damage caused directly or indirectly by the information contained in this book. For your convenience, we post an up-to-date listing of corrections on our website (ctpub.com). If a correction is not already noted, please contact our customer service department at ctinfo@ctpub.com or P.O. Box 1456, Lafayette, CA 94549.

Trademark (™) and registered trademark (®) names are used throughout this book. Rather than use the symbols with every occurrence of a trademark or registered trademark name, we are using the names only in the editorial fashion and to the benefit of the owner, with no intention of infringement.

Library of Congress Control Number: 2023936027

Printed in China

10 9 8 7 6 5 4 3

SPECIAL THANKS
Photography for this book was taken at the homes of:
Jodi Allen in Woodinville, Washington
Lori Clark of Farmhouse Cottage in Snohomish, Washington
Tracie Fish in Kenmore, Washington
Julie Smiley in Des Moines, Iowa.

Contents

Introduction

No matter how many big quilts I make, time and time again I find myself following my heart and returning to my minis. Don't get me wrong, I love a loud and proud bed quilt just as much as the next person, and among my large-project finishes are tons of lap quilts, numerous bed quilts, and not one but two king-size quilts. (If you're a quilter, I'm sure you'll agree that stitching a king quilt is pretty much the equivalent of earning a merit badge for your scout sash!)

But there are so many alternatives to traditionally large quilts. Little quilts bring endless possibilities to the table and best of all, no bed is needed! They're fun to stitch, they totally pack the adorable factor, and they tick so many boxes on my "love-of-quilting" list:

✓ No long-term commitment required; you can stitch one up knowing the finish line is in sight, and then move on to the next attractive prospect that catches your fancy.

✓ Prints can often be gathered from your scrap basket, eliminating the need to shop for more fabric. (Who are we kidding—when you finish, you can reward yourself with more fabric!)

✓ Mini projects are ideal skill builders, enabling you to try new blocks and techniques on a smaller, limited scale—if they don't give you all the cheery vibes, pat yourself on the back for trying something new and then tackle the next project on your quilting bucket list.

✓ When it comes to your home, little quilts are like a happy place waiting to happen—they can be tucked into the smallest niche to perk up a room, add a spot of color, and provide a splash of your own personal style.

✓ Small quilts are approachable and doable; you can easily whip one up for a friend and enjoy the smiles when you see that you've made their day. (Or heck, whip one up for yourself and make your own day!)

This third book of Simple Whatnots serves up a variety of techniques, an assortment of long-loved motifs, and an array of small quilts that have been among my favorites to stitch and use in my home. If big quilts are typically what's in your sewing lineup, I hope I've convinced you that good things really do come in small packages and that you'll give these petite projects a whirl.

Whether you stitch them for yourself, or stitch them for someone special in your life, quilts are truly the gift that keeps on giving.

Happy mini stitching,
~ Kim

Farmers Market

A colorful mix of prints, a boatload of pieced triangles, and strategically turned blocks all work together in perfect harmony to create this vibrant patchwork quilt featuring a strong sense of movement. Have fun with your print pairings and experiment with combinations you might normally shy away from—the results may surprise you!

MATERIALS

Yardage is based on a 42" width of useable fabric after prewashing and removing selvages.

- 2 charm squares (5" × 5") *each* of 8 assorted cream prints (combined total of 16) for blocks
- 19 chubby sixteenths (9" × 10½") of assorted print for blocks
- ½ yard of chestnut print for sashing, border, and binding
- 1 fat quarter (18" × 21") of wine print for sashing corner posts and border
- ⅔ yard of fabric for backing
- 24" × 24" square of batting

CUTTING

Cut all pieces across the width of the fabric in the order given unless otherwise noted. The cutting instructions that follow include 24 sets of assorted print patchwork pieces for the 20 blocks included in the quilt; having an extra handful of sets will give you added versatility as you choose your print pairings. If you'd prefer, you can reduce the number of sets initially cut to the 20 needed, adding additional pieces when and if they're needed as your blocks take shape.

From *each* of 8 assorted cream charm squares (1 from each print), cut:

4 squares, 1⅞" × 1⅞" (combined total of 32); cut each square in half diagonally *once* to yield 2 triangles (combined total of 64). Keep the triangles organized by print.

From the remaining 8 assorted cream charm squares, choose your 4 favorites. From *each* of these 4 charm squares, cut:

2 squares, 1⅞" × 1⅞" (combined total of 8, grand total of 40 with previously cut squares); cut each square in half diagonally *once* to yield 2 triangles (combined total of 16, grand total of 80 with previously cut squares). Keep the triangles organized by print. The remaining 4 cream charm squares will be unused.

Continued on page 8

Continued from page 7

From the 19 chubby sixteenths of assorted prints, cut a *combined total* of 24 sets (with each set cut from a single matching print) of the following:

2 squares, 1⅞" × 1⅞" (total of 24 sets, 2 matching print squares each set); cut each square in half diagonally *once* to yield 2 triangles (total of 4 per set). Keep the triangles organized by print for the half-square-triangle units.

3 squares, 1½" × 1½" (total of 24 sets, 3 matching print squares each set). Keep the squares organized by print for the diagonal center squares.

2 squares, 1½" × 1½" (total of 24 sets, 2 matching print squares each set). Keep these squares organized by print for the corner squares.

From the chestnut print, cut:

3 strips, 1" × 42"; crosscut into 24 rectangles, 1" × 3½"

2 strips, 1" × 42"; crosscut into 4 strips, 1" × 21"

3 binding strips, 2½" × 42" (for my chubby-binding method provided on page 126, reduce the strip width to 2")

From the wine print, cut:

1 strip, 1" × 21"; crosscut into 9 squares, 1" × 1"

4 strips, 3" × 21"

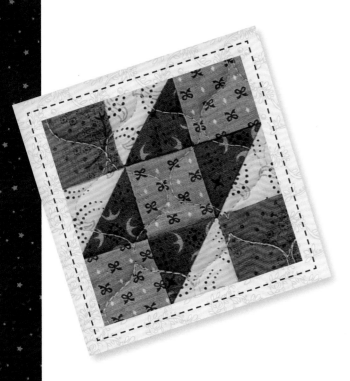

PIECING THE BLOCKS

Sew all pieces with right sides together using a ¼" seam allowance unless otherwise noted. Press the seam allowances as indicated by the arrows or as otherwise specified.

1. Select a set of four matching cream print 1⅞" triangles, four matching dark print 1⅞" triangles, three matching 1½" squares of a second dark print, and two matching 1½" squares of a third dark print.

2. Join a cream and a dark triangle along the diagonal edges. Press. Trim away the dog-ear points. Repeat to piece a total of four half-square-triangle units measuring 1½" square, including seam allowances.

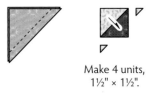

Make 4 units,
1½" × 1½".

3. Lay out the half-square-triangle units, the three squares for the diagonal center squares, and the two squares for the block corners in three horizontal rows as shown. Join the pieces in each row. Press. Join the rows. Press. The pieced block should measure 3½" square, including seam allowances.

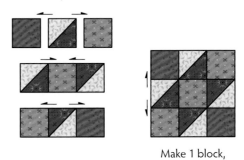

Make 1 block,
3½" × 3½".

4. Repeat steps 1–3 to piece a total of 20 blocks. Please keep in mind that if you chose to cut 24 sets of patchwork pieces to give yourself choices when choosing the prints for each block, you'll have a handful of unused sets.

Farmers Market

FINISHED QUILT SIZE: 20" × 20" ◆ FINISHED BLOCK SIZE: 3" × 3"

Designed by Kim Diehl. Pieced by Jennifer Martinez. Machine quilted by Connie Tabor.

PIECING THE QUILT CENTER

1. Referring to the illustration for block placement, lay out four blocks and three chestnut 1" × 3½" rectangles in alternating positions. Join the pieces. Press. Repeat to piece a total of four block rows measuring 3½" × 14", including seam allowances. Reserve the remaining four blocks for the border.

Make 4 block rows,
3½" × 14".

2. Lay out four chestnut 1" × 3½" rectangles and three wine 1" squares in alternating positions. Join the pieces. Press. Repeat to piece a total of three sashing rows measuring 1" × 14", including seam allowances.

Make 3 sashing rows,
1" × 14".

3. Lay out the four block rows from step 1 and the three sashing rows as shown. Join the rows. Press. The pieced quilt center should measure 14" square, including seam allowances.

Quilt center,
14" × 14".

PIECING AND ADDING THE BORDER

1. Join a chestnut 1" × 21" strip and a wine 3" × 21" strip along the long edges. Press. Crosscut this pieced strip set to make one border unit, 3½" × 14". Repeat with the remaining chestnut and wine strips to make a total of four border units.

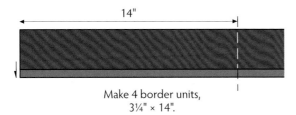

Make 4 border units, 3¼" × 14".

2. Join the chestnut edge of a border unit to the right and left side of the quilt center. Press the seam allowances toward the border units.

3. Referring to the illustration, sew a reserved block to each end of the remaining border units. Press. Join these pieced units to the remaining sides of the quilt center. Press.

Quilt assembly

COMPLETING THE QUILT

Layer and baste the quilt top, batting, and backing. The featured quilt is machine quilted with an edge-to-edge chicken wire design. Join the chestnut binding strips to make one length and use it to bind the quilt.

Wind Spinner

Easily stitched flying-geese units and basic half-square triangles take flight in this pieced mini reminiscent of my favorite spinning wind sculpture. Bold red prints anchor the patchwork design, and a supporting cast of scrappy prints rounds out the color scheme and creates a vibrant fabric garden that will forever be in bloom.

MATERIALS

Yardage is based on a 42" width of useable fabric after prewashing and removing selvages.

+ ½ yard of cream print for patchwork
+ 1 fat quarter (18" × 21") of red print #1 for patchwork and binding
+ 3 chubby sixteenths (9" × 10½") of assorted red prints for patchwork
+ 21 chubby sixteenths of assorted prints for patchwork
+ ¾ yard of fabric for backing
+ 27" × 27" square of batting

CUTTING

Cut all pieces across the width of the fabric in the order given unless otherwise noted.

From the cream print, cut:
1 strip, 4½" × 42"; crosscut into 8 squares, 4½" × 4½"
1 strip, 2½" × 42"; crosscut into 16 squares, 2½" × 2½"
1 strip, 2⅞" × 42"; from this strip, cut:
    4 squares, 2⅞" × 2⅞"; cut each square in half diagonally *once* to yield 2 triangles (total of 8)
    16 squares, 1½" × 1½"
2 strips, 1½" × 42"; crosscut into 24 rectangles, 1½" × 2½"

From red print #1, cut:
1 rectangle, 4½" × 8½"
5 binding strips, 2½" × 21" (for my chubby-binding method provided on page 126, reduce the strip width to 2")
Reserve the remainder of red print #1.

From *each* of the 3 red chubby sixteenths, cut:
1 rectangle, 4½" × 8½" (combined total of 3)
Reserve the remainder of the 3 red chubby sixteenths.

For the quilt-center patchwork (excluding the large red flying-geese triangles), from the 21 assorted print chubby sixteenths, cut a *combined total* of:
4 squares, 4½" × 4½"
4 rectangles, 2½" × 4½"
8 squares, 2⅞" × 2⅞"; cut each square in half diagonally *once* to yield 2 triangles (combined total of 16). Please note that for a scrappier look, only one triangle from each square will be used; if desired, the number of squares cut can be reduced to 4, for a combined total of 8 triangles.
8 rectangles, 1½" × 2½"
Reserve the remainder of the 21 assorted print chubby sixteenths.

From the remainder of all reserved prints (excluding cream), cut a *combined total* of:
12 squares, 2½" × 2½"
48 squares, 1½" × 1½", in matching pairs of 2 squares (24 pairs for the border flying-geese units)
48 squares, 1½" × 1½" (for the border four-patch units)

3. Repeat step 2 using the four assorted print 2½" × 4½" rectangles and the eight prepared cream 2½" squares to piece a total of four medium flying-geese units measuring 2½" × 4½", including seam allowances.

Make 4 medium units,
2½" × 4½".

4. Repeat step 2 using the eight assorted print 1½" × 2½" rectangles and the 16 prepared cream 1½" squares to piece a total of eight small flying-geese units measuring 1½" × 2½", including seam allowances.

Make 8 small units,
1½" × 2½".

PIECING THE QUILT-CENTER FLYING-GEESE UNITS

Sew all pieces with right sides together using a ¼" seam allowance unless otherwise noted. Press the seam allowances as indicated by the arrows or as otherwise specified.

1. Use a pencil and an acrylic ruler to draw a diagonal sewing line from corner to corner on the wrong side of the eight cream 4½" squares, four assorted print 4½" squares, eight of the cream 2½" squares, the 16 cream 1½" squares, and the 24 pairs of assorted print 1½" squares cut for the border flying-geese units. Reserve the four prepared assorted print 4½" squares and the 24 pairs of prepared assorted print 1½" squares for later use.

2. Select one of the red 4½" × 8½" rectangles and two prepared cream 4½" squares. Layer a prepared cream square onto one end of the red rectangle. Stitch the pair together along the drawn diagonal line. Fold the resulting inner cream triangle open, aligning the corner with the corner of the rectangle. Press. Trim away the layers beneath the top triangle, leaving a ¼" seam allowance. In the same manner, add a mirror-image cream triangle to the other end of the red rectangle. Repeat using the remaining red 4½" × 8½" rectangles and the prepared cream 4½" squares for a total of four pieced large red flying-geese units measuring 4½" × 8½", including seam allowances.

PIECING THE TRIANGLE BLOCKS

1. Join an assorted print and a cream 2⅞" triangle along the long diagonal edges. Press. Trim away the dog-ear points. Repeat for a total of eight pieced half-square-triangle units measuring 2½" square, including seam allowances. Please note that if you chose to cut your triangles from eight different assorted print squares, you'll have eight leftover triangles.

Make 8 units,
2½" × 2½".

2. Join a cream 2½" square to the dark edge of a half-square triangle as shown. Press. Join a second cream 2½" square to the adjacent dark edge of the unit. Press. Repeat to piece a total of four triangle patchwork units.

Make 4 units.

Make 4 large units,
4½" × 8½".

Wind Spinner

FINISHED QUILT SIZE: 20½" × 20½" • FINISHED BLOCK SIZE: 8" × 8"
Designed and pieced by Kim Diehl. Machine quilted by Connie Tabor.

3. Layer a reserved prepared assorted print 4½" square onto the step 2 unit. Stitch the pair together along the drawn diagonal line. Fold the resulting large triangle open as shown. Press. Trim away the layers beneath the large triangle, leaving a ¼" seam allowance. Repeat to piece a total of four double-triangle units measuring 4½" × 4½", including seam allowances.

Make 4 units,
4½" × 4½".

4. Choosing the prints randomly, join two small flying-geese units as shown. Press. Repeat for a total of four joined small flying-geese units measuring 2½" square, including seam allowances.

Make 4 units,
2½" × 2½".

5. Lay out one medium flying-geese unit, one half-square-triangle unit, and one joined small flying-geese unit in two horizontal rows. Join the pieces in the

bottom row. Press. Join the rows. Press. Repeat to piece a total of four quadruple-triangle units measuring 4½" square, including seam allowances.

Make 4 units,
4½" × 4½".

6. Lay out one quadruple-triangle unit, one double-triangle unit from step 3, and one large red flying-geese unit in two horizontal rows as shown. Join the units in the bottom row. Press. Join the rows. Press. Repeat to piece a total of four triangle blocks measuring 8½" square, including seam allowances.

 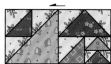 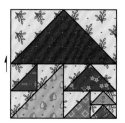

Make 4 blocks,
8½" × 8½".

PIECING THE QUILT CENTER

Referring to the illustration, lay out the blocks in two horizontal rows of two blocks. Join the blocks in each row. Press. Join the rows. Press. The pieced quilt center should measure 16½" square, including seam allowances.

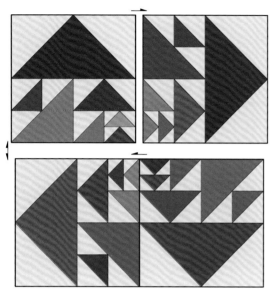

Quilt center,
16½" × 16½"

PIECING AND ADDING THE BORDER

1. Using the reserved pairs of prepared assorted print 1½" squares and the cream 1½" × 2½" rectangles, repeat step 2 of "Piecing the Quilt-Center Flying-Geese Units" on page 14 to make 24 flying-geese border units measuring 1½" × 2½", including seam allowances.

Make 24 units,
1½" × 2½".

2. Join two border flying-geese units as shown. Press. Repeat to piece a total of 12 double flying-geese units measuring 2½" square, including seam allowances.

Make 12 units,
2½" × 2½".

3. Choosing the prints randomly, lay out four assorted print 1½" squares in two horizontal rows of two squares. Join the squares in each row. Press. Join the rows. Press. Repeat to piece a total of 12 four-patch units measuring 2½" square, including seam allowances.

Make 12 units,
2½" × 2½".

4. Referring to the illustration, lay out two four-patch units, three double flying-geese units from step 2, and three assorted print 2½" squares. Join the pieces. Press. Repeat to piece a total of four pieced border strips measuring 2½" × 16½", including seam allowances.

Make 4 strips,
2½" × 16½".

5. Using the pictured quilt on page 15 as a guide, join border strips to the right and left sides of the quilt center. Press the seam allowances away from the quilt center. Join the unused four-patch units to each end of the remaining border strips. Press the seam allowances away from the newly added four-patch units. Join these completed strips to the remaining sides of the quilt center. Press the seam allowances away from the quilt center.

COMPLETING THE QUILT

Layer and baste the quilt top, batting, and backing. The featured quilt is machine quilted with an edge-to-edge design of meandering feathers. Join the red print #1 binding strips to make one length and use it to bind the quilt.

Autumn Tapestry

Prints in rich harvest colors, along with a handful of brighter hues for contrast and sparkle, are showcased in simply stitched appliqué blocks framing this medallion-style quilt. Add show-stealing oak leaves and a sprinkling of stars as the centerpiece of your design, and autumn will most definitely be in the air.

MATERIALS

Yardage is based on a 42" width of useable fabric after prewashing and removing selvages.

+ 1 fat quarter (18" × 21") of red print for blocks and binding
+ 23 chubby sixteenths (9" × 10½") of assorted prints for blocks
+ 1 fat quarter of cream print #1 for blocks
+ 3 fat eighths (9" × 21") of assorted cream prints for blocks
+ ¾ yard of fabric for backing
+ 25" × 25" square of batting
+ Freezer paper
+ Fabric glue stick
+ Water-soluble fabric glue
+ Supplies for your favorite appliqué method

CUTTING

Cut all pieces across the width of the fabric in the order given unless otherwise noted. Cutting instructions for the appliqués are provided separately.

From the red print, cut:
4 binding strips, 2½" × 21" (for my chubby-binding method provided on page 126, reduce the strip width to 2")
1 square, 6" × 6"
6 squares, 1¾" × 1¾"
Reserve the remainder of the red print.

From *each* of the 23 assorted prints, cut:
6 squares, 1¾" × 1¾" (combined total of 138)
Reserve the remainder of the assorted prints.

From cream print #1, cut:
4 squares, 3½" × 3½"
18 squares, 2½" × 2½"

From *each* of the assorted cream prints, cut:
18 squares, 2½" × 2½" (combined total of 54, grand total of 72 with previously cut squares)

CUTTING AND APPLIQUÉING THE A BLOCKS

Step-by-step instructions for my invisible machine-appliqué method begin on page 121, or you can substitute your own favorite method.

1. Using the quarter-circle pattern on page 25, trace 144 quarter-circle pattern pieces onto the dull, nonwaxy side of the freezer paper and cut them out exactly on drawn lines.

2. Using the prepared freezer-paper pattern pieces, apply a small amount of fabric glue stick to the center of the dull, nonwaxy side of each piece. Affix six pieces to the wrong side of the red print reserved in cutting and each of the remaining reserved assorted prints (combined total of 144); space the shapes approximately 1" apart.

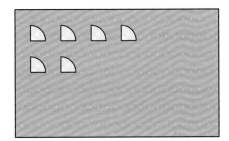

Maximizing Your Prints

While most of the quarter-circle appliqués in the featured quilt were cut with the straight edges of the pattern piece positioned on the straight grain of the cloth, I chose to cut a handful of my appliqués with the straight edges positioned diagonally on some of the directional prints. This was a quick and easy step, and it added another layer of interest to the blocks in my quilt.

3. Use scissors to cut out each piece, adding a ¼" seam allowance to the curved edge of each appliqué, and leaving an approximate ½" seam allowance (just estimate this!) along each straight edge.

¼"

4. Use a rotary cutter and acrylic ruler to trim the fabric along the straight edges to ¼", measuring out from the paper pattern pieces.

¼"

¼"

5. Use a hot, dry iron to press the curved seam allowance of each appliqué over onto the waxy side of the freezer-paper pattern. Leave the straight edge of the appliqués unpressed; they'll be enclosed within the seam allowances of the patchwork when the blocks are joined.

6. Randomly choose a cream 2½" square and four prepared quarter-circle appliqués. Dot the curved seam allowance on the wrong side of each appliqué with liquid fabric glue; affix the glue-basted pieces to the corners of the cream square, aligning the straight raw edges with the edges of the cream square. From the wrong side of the square, use a hot, dry iron to heat set the appliqués. Repeat to glue baste a total of 36 A blocks measuring 2½" square, including seam allowances.

Block A.
Make 36 blocks,
2½" × 2½".

7. Use your favorite appliqué method to stitch the curved edge *only* of the quarter-circle appliqués. Remove the freezer-paper pattern pieces through the open block corners.

FINISHED QUILT SIZE: 18½" × 18½"
FINISHED MEDALLION BLOCK SIZE: 6" × 6" ✦ FINISHED A AND B BLOCK SIZES: 2" × 2"

Designed, appliquéd, and pieced by Kim Diehl. Machine quilted by Rebecca Silbaugh.

Piecing the Four-Patch Units for the B Blocks

Sew all pieces with right sides together using a ¼" seam allowance unless otherwise noted. Press the seam allowances as indicated by the arrows or as otherwise specified.

1. Choosing randomly from the assorted prints, including the red print, join two 1¾" squares. Press. Repeat for a total of 72 joined pairs.

Make 72 units,
1¾" × 3".

2. Join two pairs from step 1 as shown. Press. Repeat to piece a total of 36 four-patch units measuring 3" square, including seam allowances.

Make 36 units,
3" × 3".

Appliquéing the B Blocks

1. Using the large circle pattern on page 25, trace and cut out 36 circle pattern pieces from freezer paper. Fold each freezer-paper circle in half and finger-press a horizontal center crease; unfold and then refold each circle to finger-press a vertical crease.

2. Apply a small amount of fabric glue stick to the center of the dull, nonwaxy side of a prepared freezer-paper circle. Align the creases in the freezer paper with the seams of a pieced four-patch unit to perfectly center it and then affix it to the wrong side of the patchwork unit. Repeat with the remaining freezer-paper circles and four-patch units.

3. Cut out each circle appliqué, adding a generous ¼" seam allowance. (A generous ¼" seam allowance will help the fabric adhere well to the paper pattern piece when the appliqué is pressed.) Use a hot, dry iron to press the seam allowance of each circle onto the waxy side of the pattern piece.

4. With right sides together, fold a cream 2½" square in half and use a hot, dry iron to press a horizontal center crease. Unfold and then refold the square to press a vertical center crease. Repeat with the remaining cream 2½" squares.

5. Dot the seam allowance on the wrong side of a circle appliqué with liquid basting glue. Align the seams of the appliqué with the pressed creases of the cream square to perfectly center it and then affix it to the square. Heat set the appliqué as previously instructed. Repeat to glue baste a total of 36 B blocks.

Block B.
Make 36 blocks,
2½" × 2½".

6. Use your favorite appliqué method to stitch each appliqué in place. From the wrong side of each block, cut away the center of the stitched circle ¼" in from the line of stitching and remove the paper pattern pieces.

APPLIQUÉING THE CENTER MEDALLION BLOCK

1. Using the patterns provided on page 25 and your favorite appliqué method, cut and prepare the following pieces.

- 1 four-branched oak leaf from the 6" square of red print
- 4 small leaves from the scraps of green print*
- 4 stars from the scraps of dark gold print*
- 1 small center circle from the scraps of a second green print*

Or choose your own favorite prints!

2. Lay out the four 3½" cream print #1 squares in two horizontal rows of two squares each to make a four-patch unit, positioning the print as shown in the featured quilt on page 21 if your print is directional. Join the pieces in each row. Press the seam allowances of each row in opposite directions. Join the rows. Press the seam allowances to one side. The pieced square should measure 6½" square, including seam allowances.

3. Stitch the four-branched oak-leaf appliqué onto the center of the pieced cream square. Next, position and stitch the small green leaves and small center circle onto the stitched oak-leaf appliqué. Last, stitch the four gold stars in place.

PIECING THE QUILT TOP

1. Using the pictured quilt on page 21 and the quilt assembly diagram on page 24 as a guide, lay out five A blocks and four B blocks in alternating positions. Join the blocks. Press. Repeat to make a total of four A rows measuring 2½" × 18½", including seam allowances.

2. Using five B blocks and four A blocks for each row, repeat step 1 to make a total of two B rows measuring 2½" × 18½", including seam allowances.

3. Lay out two B blocks and one A block in alternating positions. Join the blocks. Repeat to make a total of four C rows measuring 2½" × 6½", including seam allowances.

4. Using two A blocks and one B block for each row, repeat step 3 to make a total of two D rows measuring 2½" × 6½", including seam allowances.

5. Join an A row to each long edge of a B row. Press. Repeat to make a total of two top and bottom block sections measuring 6½" × 18½", including seam allowances.

6. Join a C row to each long edge of a D row. Press. Repeat to make a total of two center block units measuring 6½" square, including seam allowances.

7. Join a center block unit to the right and left sides of the appliquéd medallion block. Press.

8. Join a step 5 block unit to the top and bottom long edges of the step 7 unit. Press the seam allowances away from the quilt center.

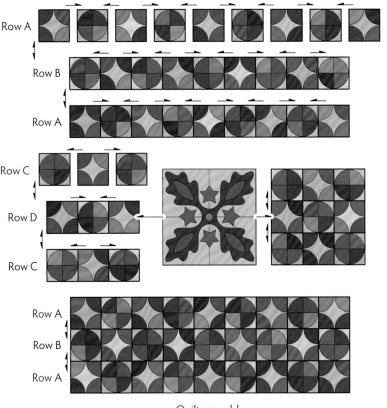

Quilt assembly

COMPLETING THE QUILT

Layer and baste the quilt top, batting, and backing. The featured quilt is machine quilted with the appliqués of the center medallion echoed to emphasize their shapes. Arced lines are stitched onto the inner curved edge of each quarter-circle appliqué and the circle appliqué quadrants. All circular appliqués are outlined to emphasize their shapes and each block is stitched in the ditch (along the seamlines). Join the red binding strips to make one length and use it to bind the quilt.

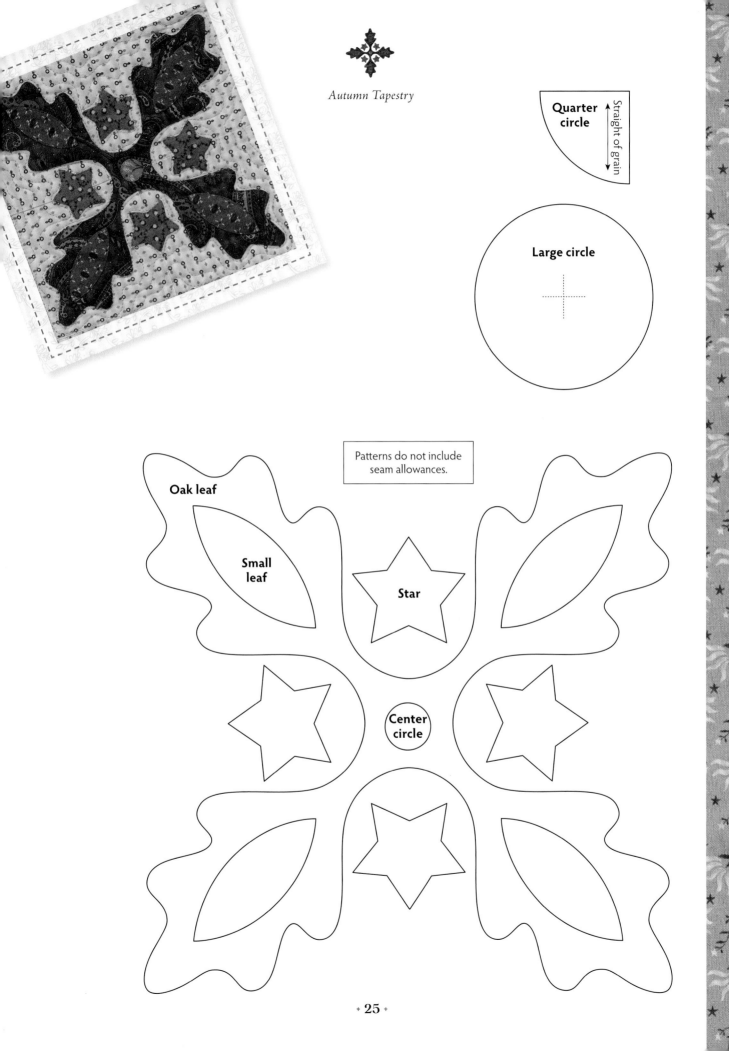

Autumn Tapestry

Quarter circle

Straight of grain

Large circle

Patterns do not include seam allowances.

Oak leaf

Small leaf

Star

Center circle

Woven Stars

Classic Star blocks with an added stitched twist bring all the happy feels when fashioned from shades of spiced pumpkin, mocha brown, and toasted marshmallow. If different hues make you happy, simply choose and substitute your own favorite colors to personalize your quilt palette and highlight your own individual style.

MATERIALS

Yardage is based on a 42" width of useable fabric after prewashing and removing selvages.

- ⅓ yard of orange print for blocks and outer border
- 1 fat eighth (9" × 21") *each* of 2 cream prints for blocks and border cornerstones
- 1 fat quarter (18" × 21") *each* of 2 brown prints for blocks, sashing, middle border, and binding
- 1 fat quarter of orange plaid or print for blocks, sashing squares, and inner border
- ⅞ yard of fabric for backing
- 29" × 29" square of batting

CUTTING

Cut all pieces across the width of the fabric in the order given unless otherwise noted.

From the orange print, cut:
2 strips, 1⅞" × 42"; crosscut into 36 squares, 1⅞" × 1⅞". Cut each square in half diagonally *once* to yield 2 triangles (total of 72).
2 strips, 3" × 42"; crosscut *each* strip into:
    1 strip, 3" × 18" (total of 2)
    1 strip, 3" × 23" (total of 2)

From cream print #1, cut:
36 squares, 1⅞" × 1⅞"; cut each square in half diagonally *once* to yield 2 triangles (total of 72)
4 squares, 1" × 1"

From cream print #2, cut:
40 squares, 1½" × 1½"
13 squares, 1" × 1"

From brown print #1, cut:
36 squares, 1½" × 1½"
5 binding strips, 2½" × 21" (for my chubby-binding method provided on page 126, reduce the strip width to 2")

From the orange plaid or print, cut:
36 rectangles, 1" × 2½"
12 squares, 1½" × 1½"
4 strips, 1" × 16"

From brown print #2, cut:
24 rectangles, 1½" × 2¼"
4 strips, 1" × 17"

Piecing the Blocks

*Sew all pieces with right sides together using a ¼"
seam allowance unless otherwise noted. Press the seam
allowances as indicated by the arrows or as otherwise
specified.*

1. Join cream print #1 and orange print 1⅞" triangles
along the long diagonal edges. Press. Trim away the
dog-ear points. Repeat to piece a total of 72 half-
square-triangle units measuring 1½" square, including
seam allowances.

Make 72 units,
1½" × 1½".

2. Lay out two half-square-triangle units, one 1½"
cream print #2 square, and one 1½" brown print #1
square in two horizontal rows as shown. Join the pieces

in each row. Press. Join the rows. Press. Repeat to piece
a total of 36 block corner units measuring 2½" square,
including seam allowances.

Make 36 units,
2½" × 2½".

3. Lay out two orange plaid 1" × 2½" rectangles and
one 1" cream print #2 square in alternating positions.
Join the pieces. Press. Repeat to piece a total of nine
block center-row units measuring 1" × 5", including
seam allowances.

Make 9 units,
1" × 5".

4. Join a block corner unit to each long side of an orange 1" × 2½" rectangle as shown. Press. Repeat to piece a total of 18 block outer-row units measuring 2½" × 5", including seam allowances.

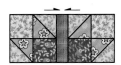

Make 18 units,
2½" × 5".

5. Join a block outer-row unit to each long side of a block center-row unit. Press. Repeat to piece a total of nine Star blocks measuring 5" square, including seam allowances.

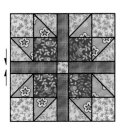

Make 9 blocks,
5" × 5".

◆ EXTRA SNIPPET ◆

Triangles on Top

When I'm stitching block components that include pieced triangles, I've learned to pin them together with the triangle unit as the topmost layer. This enables me to see the triangle seams as I feed the pinned patchwork under the sewing-machine needle, and I can easily guide the unit in such a way that the seamline will land right in the sweet spot and produce beautifully sharp points.

PIECING THE QUILT CENTER

Please refer to the quilt assembly diagram below as a guide for the steps that follow.

1. Sew a 1½" × 2¼" brown print #2 rectangle to each opposite side of an orange plaid 1½" square. Press. Repeat to piece a total of 12 sashing rectangles measuring 1½" × 5", including seam allowances.

Make 12 units,
1½" × 5".

2. Referring to the quilt assembly diagram, lay out three Star blocks and two sashing units in alternating positions. Join the pieces. Repeat to piece a total of three block rows measuring 5" × 16", including seam allowances.

3. Lay out three sashing units and two 1½" cream print #2 squares in alternating positions as shown below. Join the pieces. Repeat to piece a total of two sashing rows measuring 1½" x 16", including seam allowances.

4. Lay out the three block rows from step 2 and the two sashing rows in alternating positions. Join the rows. The pieced quilt center should measure 16" square, including seam allowances.

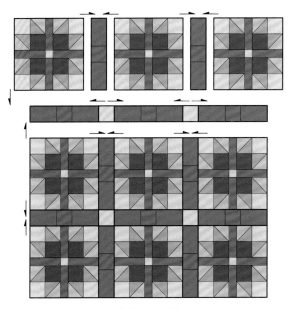

Quilt assembly

FINISHED QUILT SIZE: 23" × 23" ◆ FINISHED BLOCK SIZE: 4½" × 4½"

Designed by Kim Diehl. Pieced by Jennifer Martinez. Machine quilted by Rebecca Silbaugh.

ADDING THE BORDERS

1. Referring to the illustration below, join an orange plaid 1" × 16" inner-border strip to the right and left sides of the quilt center. Press. Sew a 1" cream print #1 square to each end of the remaining orange plaid strips. Press. Join these pieced strips to the remaining sides of the quilt center. Press. The quilt top should now measure 17" square, including seam allowances.

2. Using the four 1" × 17" brown print #2 strips and the four 1" cream print #2 squares, repeat step 1 to add the middle-border strips to the quilt top, bringing the measurement to 18" square, including seam allowances.

3. Join the orange 3" × 18" strips to the right and left sides of the quilt top. Press. Join the orange 3" × 23" strips to the remaining sides of the quilt top. Press.

COMPLETING THE QUILT

Layer and baste the quilt top, batting, and backing. The featured quilt is machine quilted with a feathered wreath stitched onto each Star block, and the blocks are stitched in the ditch (along the outer seamlines). The brown sashing rectangles are quilted with elongated Xs, and Xs are stitched onto each orange plaid and cream 1½" sashing square. The inner and middle borders are stitched with a ribbon candy design that crosses the center horizontal seam to unify them into one pieced row, and the inner and outer seams of these rows (not the center seam) are stitched in the ditch. The outer border is stitched with a diagonal 1" crosshatch design. Join the brown #1 binding strips to make one length and use it to bind the quilt.

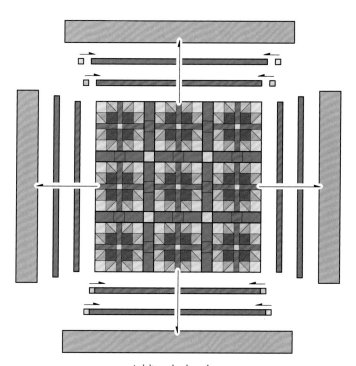

Adding the borders

Charm School

Humble Nine Patch blocks are often among the first we learn to stitch because they're so approachable and doable. This easily sewn block is also incredibly versatile—stitch it from two complementary colors for a traditional look, or instantly create the look of a checkerboard by raiding your scrap basket and using all the colors in the rainbow.

MATERIALS

Yardage is based on a 42" width of useable fabric after prewashing and removing selvages.

- ¼ yard (not a fat quarter) of cream print #1 for blocks, setting squares, and border
- 3 fat eighths (9" × 21") of assorted cream prints for blocks, setting squares, and border
- ½ yard of teal print for blocks, border, and binding
- 24 charm squares (5" × 5") of assorted prints for blocks
- ¾ yard of fabric for backing
- 27" × 34" rectangle of batting

CUTTING

Cut all pieces across the width of the fabric in the order given unless otherwise noted.

From cream print #1, cut:
2 strips, 1" × 42"; crosscut *each* strip into:
  1 strip, 1" × 21½" (total of 2)
  1 strip, 1" × 15½" (total of 2)
Reserve the remainder of cream print #1.

From the 3 assorted cream prints and the remainder of cream print #1, cut a *combined total* of:
11 squares, 3½" × 3½"
20 sets of 4 squares, 1½" × 1½", with each set cut from a *single* matching cream print (combined total of 80)

From the teal print, cut:
4 strips, 1¾" × 42"; crosscut *each* strip into:
  1 strip, 1¾ × 21½" (total of 4)
  1 strip, 1¾" × 15½" (total of 4)
3 binding strips, 2½" × 42" (for my chubby-binding method provided on page 126, reduce the strip width to 2")
Reserve the remainder of the teal print.

From the 24 charm squares of assorted prints (referred to collectively as "dark"), cut a *combined total* of:
20 sets of 5 squares, 1½" × 1½", with each set cut from a single matching print (combined total of 100)
Reserve the scraps of the dark squares.

From the remainder of the teal print and the remainder of the 24 dark scraps, cut a *combined total* of:
72 squares, 1½" × 1½"

PIECING THE NINE PATCH BLOCKS

Sew all pieces with right sides together using a ¼" seam allowance unless otherwise noted. Press the seam allowances as indicated by the arrows or as otherwise specified.

1. Select a matching set of four 1½" squares cut from a single cream print and a matching set of five 1½" squares cut from a single dark print.

2. Referring to the illustration, lay out the squares in three horizontal rows of three squares. Join the squares in each row. Press. Join the rows. Press. Repeat to piece a total of 20 Nine Patch blocks measuring 3½" square, including seam allowances.

Make 20 blocks,
3½" × 3½".

♦ EXTRA SNIPPET ♦

When Short Is Good

When stitching small-scale patchwork like the Nine Patch and Checkerboard blocks featured in this quilt, experience has taught me to shorten the stitch length on my sewing machine (for my machine, I reduce the length from a setting of 2.2 to 1.8). One benefit to a reduced stitch length is that your joined patchwork will stay joined from edge to edge, without being prone to pulling apart at the ends. A second benefit is that for blocks or units with seam allowances that have been pressed open (enabling them to nest together, regardless of the direction of the seams they'll be joined to), your stitches will remain invisible and secure.

PIECING THE CHECKERBOARD BLOCKS

Choosing the prints randomly, select nine assorted dark print 1½" squares. Lay out the squares in three horizontal rows of three squares. Join the squares in each row. Press. Join the rows. Press. Repeat to piece a total of eight Checkerboard blocks measuring 3½" square, including seam allowances.

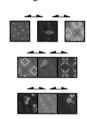

Make 8 blocks,
3½" × 3½".

PIECING THE QUILT CENTER

Referring to the quilt assembly diagram, lay out 16 pieced Nine Patch blocks, eight pieced Checkerboard blocks, and 11 assorted cream 3½" squares in seven horizontal rows. Join the pieces in each row. Press. Join the rows. Press. The pieced quilt center should measure 15½" × 21½", including seam allowances. Reserve the remaining four Nine Patch blocks for the border.

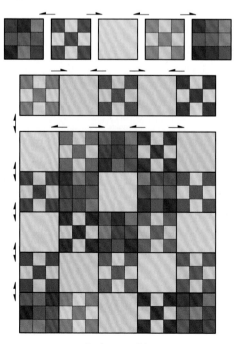

Quilt assembly

FINISHED QUILT SIZE: 21½" × 27½" ✦ **FINISHED BLOCK SIZE: 3" × 3"**

Designed, pieced, and machine quilted by Kim Diehl.

Piecing and Adding the Border

1. Join a teal 1¾" × 21½" strip to each long side of a cream 1" × 21½" strip. Press the seam allowances toward the teal strips. Repeat to piece a total of two pieced long border strips measuring 3½" × 21½", including seam allowances. Join these border strips to the right and left sides of the quilt center. Press the seam allowances toward the teal border strips.

Make 2 side borders,
3½" × 21½".

2. Join a teal 1¾" × 15½" strip to each long side of a cream 1" × 15½" strip. Press the seam allowances toward the teal strips. Repeat to make a total of two short border strips measuring 3½" × 15½", including seam allowances. Join a reserved Nine Patch block to

each end of the two short border strips. Press the seam allowances toward the border strips. Join these borders to the top and bottom edges of the quilt top. Press the seam allowances toward the borders.

Make 2 top/bottom borders,
3½" × 15½".

Completing the Quilt

Layer and baste the quilt top, batting, and backing. The featured quilt is machine quilted with an orange-peel design on the pieced and cream squares. The border strips are stitched with a diagonal crosshatch design. Join the teal binding strips to make one length and use it to bind the quilt.

Pint Size

Framed checkerboard squares come together in a jiffy and take on a unique look when framed with light and dark strips in this scrappy mini quilt. To simplify gathering and cutting your fabrics, a specified number of prints have been suggested, but if you're blessed with a generous stash of scraps, pull out all the stops and slide them into your lineup!

MATERIALS

Yardage is based on a 42"-width of useable fabric after prewashing and removing selvages.

- 1 fat quarter (18" × 21") of brown print for blocks and binding
- 23 chubby sixteenths (9" × 10½") of assorted prints for blocks
- 4 fat eighths (9" × 21") of assorted cream prints for blocks
- ¾ yard of fabric for backing
- 27" × 27" square of batting

CUTTING

Cut all pieces across the width of the fabric in the order given unless otherwise noted.

From the brown print, cut:
5 binding strips, 2½" × 21" (for my chubby-binding method provided on page 126, reduce the strip width to 2")
Reserve the remainder of the brown print.

From *each* of the assorted prints and the reserved brown print, cut:
9 squares, 1½" × 1½" (combined total of 216)
Reserve the assorted print scraps.

From the remainder of the assorted print scraps, cut a *total* of 13 matching sets of:
2 rectangles, 1" × 3½" (combined total of 26)
2 rectangles, 1" × 4½" (combined total of 26)

From *each* of the assorted cream prints, cut:
6 rectangles, 1" × 3½" (combined total of 24)
6 rectangles, 1" × 4½" (combined total of 24)
6 squares, 1½" × 1½" (combined total of 24)
Reserve the scraps of one assorted cream print.

From the reserved cream scraps, cut:
1 square, 1½" × 1½"

PIECING THE BLOCKS

*Sew all pieces with right sides together using a ¼"
seam allowance unless otherwise noted. Press the seam
allowances as indicated by the arrows or as otherwise
specified.*

1. Randomly select eight assorted print 1½" squares
and one cream 1½" square, including the brown print
squares with the assorted prints. Lay out the squares in
three horizontal rows of three squares each, placing the
cream print in the center of the middle row. Join the
squares in each row. Press. Join the rows. Press. Repeat
to piece a total of 25 nine-patch units measuring 3½"
square, including seam allowances. Please note that
you'll have 16 unused assorted print squares; these
have been included for added choices as you piece the
blocks.

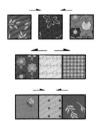

Make 25 units,
3½" × 3½".

2. Select one set of matching assorted print
rectangles. Join the 1" × 3½" rectangles to the right and
left sides of a nine-patch unit. Press. Join the 1" × 4½"

rectangles to the remaining edges of the nine-patch
unit. Press. Repeat to make a total of 13 Dark Framed
blocks measuring 4½" square, including seam
allowances.

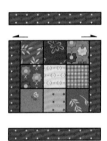
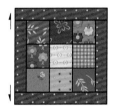

Make 13 Dark Framed blocks,
4½" × 4½".

3. Join matching cream print 1" × 3½" rectangles
to the left and right sides of a remaining nine-patch
unit. Press. Join matching 1" × 4½" rectangles of the
same print as the side rectangles to the top and bottom
of the nine-patch unit. Press. Repeat to make a total
of 12 Cream Framed blocks measuring 4½" square,
including seam allowances.

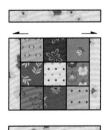
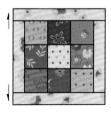

Make 12 Cream Framed blocks,
4½" × 4½".

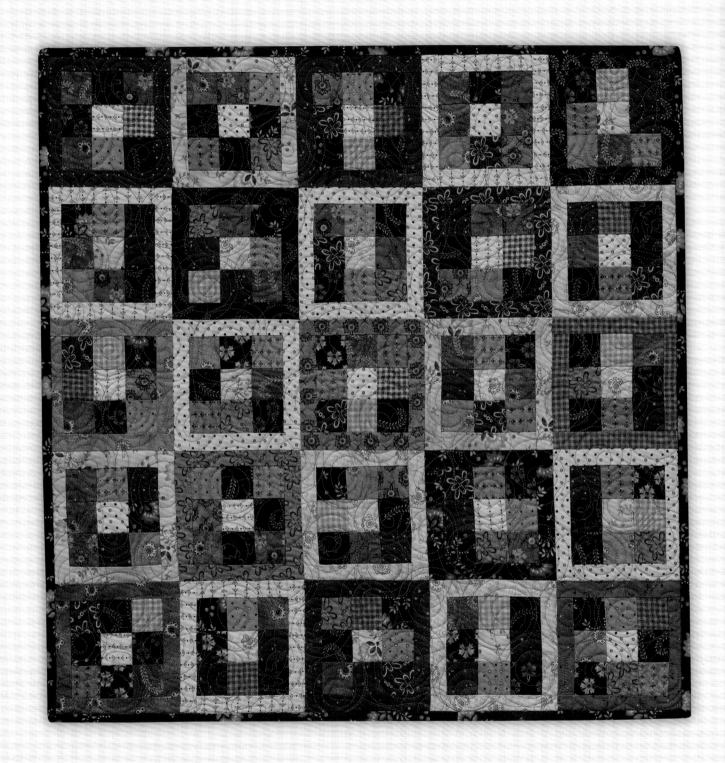

FINISHED QUILT SIZE: 20½" × 20½" ✦ FINISHED BLOCK SIZE: 4" × 4"

Designed and pieced by Kim Diehl. Machine quilted by Deborah Poole.

Pint Size

PIECING THE QUILT TOP

Referring to the quilt assembly diagram, lay out the pieced blocks in five horizontal rows of five, alternating the placement of the cream and dark blocks in each row. Place the dark blocks so the sides without seams are at the top and bottom; rotate the cream blocks so the sides without seams are on the sides. (This will allow the seams to nest together when joined.) Join the blocks in each row. Press. Join the rows.

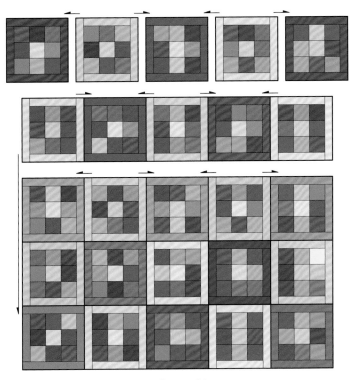

Quilt assembly

COMPLETING THE QUILT

Layer and baste the quilt top, batting, and backing. The featured quilt is machine quilted with an overall swirling design that resembles cinnamon rolls. Join the brown binding strips to make one length and use it to bind the quilt.

Apple Baskets

A tisket, a tasket, red and black baskets! Small-scale prints are absolutely ideal for this sweet mini, and the classic baskets and flying-geese patchwork in rich shades of inky black and apple red form delightful secondary patterns— the more you look, the more you see!

MATERIALS

Yardage is based on a 42" width of useable fabric after prewashing and removing selvages.

- 1 fat eighth (9" × 21") *each of cream prints #1 and #2 for blocks and sashing*
- 1 fat quarter (18" × 21") *each of black prints #1 and #2 for blocks, sashing, border, and binding*
- 1 chubby sixteenth (9" × 10½") *each of red prints #1, #2, and #3 for blocks, sashing, and border*
- 2 charm squares (5" × 5") of assorted red prints for sashing
- ⅔ yard of fabric for backing
- 23" × 23" square of batting

CUTTING

Cut all pieces across the width of the fabric in the order given unless otherwise noted.

From cream print #1, cut:
3 strips, 1½" × 21"; crosscut into:
    8 rectangles, 1½" × 2½"
    4 squares, 1½" × 1½"
    8 rectangles, 1½" × 3½"
1 strip, 2½" × 21"; crosscut into 4 squares, 2½" × 2½".
    From the remainder of this strip, cut 4 squares,
    1⅞" × 1⅞". Cut each square in half diagonally *once*
    to yield 2 triangles (total of 8).

From cream print #2, cut:
1 strip, 3½" × 21"; crosscut into 4 squares, 3½" × 3½"
3 strips, 1½" × 21"; crosscut into 20 rectangles,
    1½" × 2½"

From black print #1, cut:
1 strip, 1½" × 21"; crosscut into 8 squares, 1½" × 1½"
1 strip, 1⅞" × 21"; crosscut into 4 squares, 1⅞" × 1⅞".
    Cut each square in half diagonally *once* to yield 2
    triangles (total of 8).
4 binding strips, 2½" × 21" (for my chubby-binding
    method provided on page 126, reduce the strip
    width to 2")

From *each* of red prints #1 and #2, cut:
1 rectangle, 4½" × 10½"; crosscut into 2 squares,
    4½" × 4½" (combined total of 4)
Reserve the remainder of red prints #1 and #2.

From red print #3, cut:
3 rectangles, 1½" × 10½"; crosscut into 16 squares,
    1½" × 1½"
1 rectangle, 2½" × 10½"; crosscut into 4 squares,
    2½" × 2½"

From *each* of the red print charm squares and the remainder of red prints #1 and #2, cut:
8 squares, 1½" × 1½" (combined total of 32)
Keep the squares organized by print.

From black print #2, cut:
4 strips, 2½" × 21"; crosscut into 4 rectangles,
    2½" × 12½". From the remainder of one strip,
    cut 1 square, 2½" × 2½".

Piecing the Basket Blocks

*Sew all pieces with right sides together using a ¼"
seam allowance unless otherwise noted. Press the seam
allowances as indicated by the arrows or as otherwise
specified.*

1. Use a pencil and an acrylic ruler to draw a diagonal
sewing line from corner to corner on the wrong side of
the eight 1½" black print #1 squares, the two 4½" red
print #1 squares, the two 4½" red print #2 squares, and
the four 2½" cream print #1 squares.

2. Layer a prepared 1½" black print #1 square onto
one end of a 1½" × 2½" cream print #1 rectangle as
shown. Stitch the pair together along the drawn line.
Fold the resulting inner black triangle open, aligning
the corner with the corner of the cream rectangle.
Press. Trim away the layers beneath the top triangle,
leaving a ¼" seam allowance. Repeat to piece a total
of four half-flying-geese units and four mirror-image
half-flying-geese units measuring 1½" × 2½", including
seam allowances.

Make 4 of each unit,
1½" × 2½".

3. Join a 1⅞" cream print #1 and a black print #1
triangle along the long diagonal edges. Press. Trim
away the dog-ear points. Repeat to piece a total of eight
half-square-triangle units measuring 1½" square,
including seam allowances.

Make 8 units,
1½" × 1½".

4. Join a half-square-triangle unit to a half-flying-
geese unit from step 2 as shown. Press. Repeat to piece
a total of four basket-point units and four mirror-
image basket-point units measuring 1½" × 3½",
including seam allowances.

Make 4 of each unit,
1½" × 3½".

5. Referring to the illustration, lay out a basket-point unit, a mirror-image basket-point unit, one 1½" cream print #1 square, and one 3½" cream print #2 square in two horizontal rows. Join the pieces in each row. Press. Join the rows. Press. Repeat to piece a total of four basket-top units measuring 4½" square, including seam allowances.

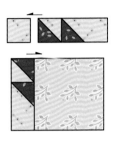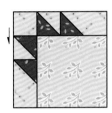

Make 4 units,
4½" × 4½".

6. Select a prepared 4½" red print #1 square. Using the illustration as a guide, layer the red square onto a basket-top unit. Pin the units together along the drawn diagonal line. Stitch the pieces together along the line. Fold the resulting red triangle open as shown, aligning the corner with the corner of the basket-top unit. Press. Trim away the layers beneath the top red triangle, leaving a ¼" seam allowance. Repeat using the remaining prepared red 4½" square, to piece four red and black basket units measuring 4½" square, including seam allowances.

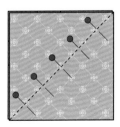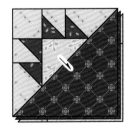

Make 4 units,
4½" × 4½".

7. Join a 1½" red print #3 square to one end of a 1½" × 3½" cream print #1 rectangle. Press. Repeat to piece a total of eight pieced rectangles measuring 1½" × 4½", including seam allowances. Reserve the remaining 1½" red print #3 squares for later use.

Make 8 units,
1½" × 4½".

8. Join a pieced rectangle to a red and black basket unit from step 6 as shown. Press. Join a second pieced rectangle to the adjacent red corner of the unit. Press. Repeat to piece a total of four footed basket units measuring 5½" square (minus the open corner), including seam allowances.

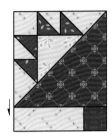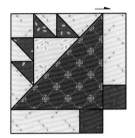

9. Add a 2½" cream print #1 square to the corner of the basket unit as previously instructed. Repeat to piece a total of four Basket blocks measuring 5½" square, including seam allowances.

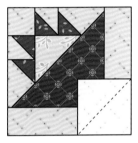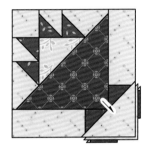

Make 4 blocks,
5½" × 5½".

PIECING THE FLYING-GEESE SASHING UNITS

1. Draw a diagonal sewing line on the wrong side of each of the 32 assorted red 1½" squares and the reserved 1½" red print #3 squares as previously instructed.

2. Select one 1½" × 2½" cream print #2 rectangle and two prepared matching red 1½" squares. Referring to step 2 of "Piecing the Basket Blocks" on page 44, piece a red flying-geese unit measuring 1½" × 2½", including seam allowances. Repeat to piece a total of 20 red flying-geese units, with four units pieced from each of the five red prints.

Make 20 units,
1½" × 2½".

FINISHED QUILT SIZE: 16½" × 16½" ◆ FINISHED BLOCK SIZE: 5" × 5"
Designed and pieced by Kim Diehl. Machine quilted by Connie Tabor.

3. Choosing one unit from each red print, lay out five red flying-geese units as shown. Join the units. Press. Repeat, positioning the red prints randomly, to piece a total of four flying-geese sashing units measuring 2½" × 5½", including seam allowances.

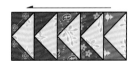

Make 4 units,
2½" × 5½".

PIECING THE QUILT CENTER

Using the assembly diagram as a guide, lay out the four Basket blocks, the four flying-geese sashing units, and the 2½" black print #2 square in three horizontal rows. Join the pieces in each row. Press. Join the rows. Press. The quilt center should measure 12½" square, including seam allowances.

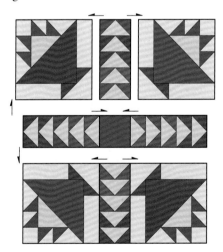

Quilt assembly

ADDING THE BORDER

Join a 2½" × 12½" black print #2 rectangle to the right and left side of the quilt center. Press. Join a 2½" red print #3 square to each end of the remaining black print #2 rectangles. Press. Join these pieced black strips to the top and bottom of the quilt center. Press.

Adding the borders

COMPLETING THE QUILT

Layer and baste the quilt top, batting, and backing. Quilt the layers. The featured quilt is machine quilted with an edge-to-edge Baptist Fan design. Join the black print #1 binding strips to make one length and use it to bind the quilt.

Slightly Tipsy

Combine scads of richly hued scraps and two flirty styles of tiny Drunkard's Path blocks, and what's the happy result? A colorful mini quilt full of movement and cheer— half patchwork, half appliqué, and completely intoxicating!

MATERIALS

Yardage is based on a 42" width of useable fabric after prewashing and removing selvages.

- 35 charm squares (5" × 5") of assorted prints for blocks and border
- 35 charm squares of assorted cream prints for blocks and border
- 1 fat quarter (18" × 21") of dark print for binding
- 1 fat quarter of fabric for backing
- 17" × 21" piece of batting
- Supplies for your favorite appliqué method

CUTTING

Cut all pieces across the width of the fabric in the order given unless otherwise noted. The quarter-circle appliqué pattern is provided on page 53, cut the pattern pieces exactly on the drawn lines the number of times specified below, adding a ¼" seam allowance on all sides when preparing the appliqués from cloth. You may wish to cut an extra handful of appliqués from the cream and assorted prints for added choices as you stitch the blocks.

From *each* of 28 assorted print charm squares, cut:
1 rectangle, 2½" × 5"; from this rectangle, cut 1 square, 2½" × 2½" (combined total of 28), and 1 square, 1½" × 1½" (combined total of 28)
Reserve the remainder of the 28 assorted prints.

From the 7 remaining assorted print charm squares and the remainder of the 28 assorted prints, cut a combined total of:
44 squares, 1½" × 1½" (grand total of 72 with previously cut squares)
Reserve the scraps of all 35 assorted prints for the appliqués.

From the scraps of all 35 assorted prints, cut a combined total of:
68 quarter-circle appliqués

From the 35 assorted cream print charm squares, cut a combined total of:
128 squares, 1½" × 1½"
72 quarter-circle appliqués

From the dark print for binding, cut:
4 binding strips, 2½" × 21" (for my chubby-binding method on page 126, reduce the strip width to 2")

2. Repeat to appliqué a total of 72 A quarter-block units measuring 1½" square, including seam allowances.

Appliqué placement.
Make 72 A quarter-block units.

3. Select a cream 1½" square and a quarter-circle appliqué cut from one of the assorted prints. Repeat steps 1 and 2 to appliqué a total of 68 B quarter-block units measuring 1½" square, including seam allowances.

Appliqué placement.
Make 68 B quarter-block units.

APPLIQUÉING THE A AND B UNITS

Step-by-step instructions for my invisible machine-appliqué method begin on page 121, or you can substitute your own favorite method.

1. Select a prepared 1½" square from one of the assorted prints and a cream print quarter-circle appliqué. Align the straight edges of the appliqué with one corner of the darker square to position it correctly; use your favorite method to appliqué the curved edge to the background square. Do *not* turn under or trim away the seam allowances along the straight edges of the appliqué, as they will be absorbed into the seam allowances of the patchwork when the blocks are joined.

Note: If you're using my invisible machine-appliqué method, turn under and press *only* the curved appliqué edge using a freeze-paper pattern piece. Once prepared, align the straight appliqué edges with the background square corner as described above, pin or baste the appliqué in place, and stitch the curved edge to secure it to the background. Trim away the excess background fabric underneath the appliqué, leaving a ¼" seam allowance, and remove the freezer-paper pattern piece.

PIECING THE A AND B DRUNKARD'S PATH BLOCKS

1. Lay out four A quarter-block units in two horizontal rows as shown. Join the units. Press. Join the rows. Press. Repeat to piece 18 Drunkard's Path A blocks measuring 2½" square, including seam allowances.

Make 18 Drunkard's
Path A blocks,
2½" × 2½".

2. Lay out four B quarter-block units in two horizontal rows as shown. Join the units. Press. Join the rows. Press. Repeat to piece 17 Drunkard's Path B blocks measuring 2½" square, including seam allowances.

Make 17 Drunkard's
Path B blocks,
2½" × 2½".

Slightly Tipsy

FINISHED QUILT SIZE: 14½" × 18½" ✦ **FINISHED BLOCK SIZE: 2" × 2"**

Designed, pieced, and appliquéd by Kim Diehl. Machine quilted by Connie Tabor.

PIECING THE QUILT CENTER

Using the assembly diagram as a guide, lay out the Drunkard's Path A and B blocks in alternating positions in seven rows of five blocks. Join the blocks in each row. Press. Join the rows. Press. The pieced quilt center should measure 10½" × 14½", including seam allowances.

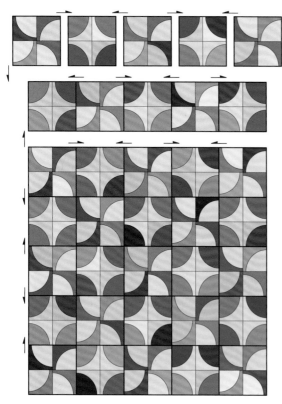

Quilt assembly

PIECING AND ADDING THE BORDER

1. Use a pencil and an acrylic ruler to draw a diagonal sewing line from corner to corner on the wrong side of each remaining cream 1½" square.

2. Select a 2½" assorted print square and two prepared cream 1½" squares. Position a cream square on one corner of the darker 2½" square as shown. Stitch the pair along the drawn diagonal line. Fold the

resulting inner cream triangle open, aligning the corner with the corner of the bottom square. Press. Trim away the layers beneath the top triangle, leaving a ¼" seam allowance. In the same manner, add a mirror-image triangle to the adjacent corner of the dark square. Repeat to piece a total of 24 border units measuring 2½" square, including seam allowances.

Make 24 border units,
2½" × 2½".

3. Select one print 2½" square and three prepared cream 1½" squares. Repeat step 2 to piece a cream triangle onto one corner of the darker square, then continue as previously instructed to add one cream triangle to the two adjacent corners. Repeat to piece a total of four border corner units measuring 2½" square, including seam allowances.

Make 4 corner units,
2½" × 2½".

4. Lay out seven border units from step 2 side by side, as shown. Join the units. Press. Repeat to piece a total of two side border rows measuring 2½" × 14½", including seam allowances. Join these rows to the right and left sides of the quilt center. Press.

Make 2 side borders,
2½" × 14½".

5. Referring to the illustration on page 53, and using five border units from step 2 and two border corner units from step 3, repeat step 4 to piece two top and bottom border rows measuring 2½" × 14½". Press. Join these rows to the remaining edges of the quilt center. Press.

Adding the borders

COMPLETING THE QUILT

Layer and baste the quilt top, batting, and backing. Quilt the layers. The featured quilt is machine quilted with vertical rows of meandering serpentine feathered vines. Join the print binding strips to make one length and use it to bind the quilt.

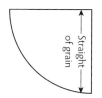

Straight
of grain

**Quarter-circle
appliqué pattern**

Frugal Farm Wife

With its sprinkling of "make-do" blocks stitched from pieced-together prints, this mini pays homage to my grandma and the quilts she stitched during lean times. Often the smallest snippets of cloth were joined together to make her needed patches, but rather than minimizing the appeal, this frugal approach only increased the charm of her quilts.

MATERIALS

Yardage is based on a 42" width of useable fabric after prewashing and removing selvages.

- 4 fat eighths (9" × 21") of assorted cream prints for blocks and border

- 1 fat quarter (18" × 21") of brown print #1 for blocks, border, and binding

- 24 chubby sixteenths (9" × 10½") of assorted prints (including brown print #2) for blocks and border

- ⅔ yard of fabric for backing

- 24" × 31" rectangle of batting

CUTTING

Cut all pieces across the width of the fabric in the order given unless otherwise noted.

From *each* of the 4 assorted cream prints, cut:
2 strips, 1½" × 21"; crosscut into 18 squares, 1½" × 1½" (combined total of 72)
Reserve the remainder of the 4 assorted cream prints.

From the remainder of the 4 assorted cream prints, cut a *combined total* of:
6 squares, 3⅞" × 3⅞"; cut each square in half diagonally *once* to yield 2 triangles (combined total of 12)

From brown print #1, cut:
1 strip, 3⅞" × 21"; crosscut into 4 squares, 3⅞" × 3⅞". Cut each square in half diagonally *once* to yield 2 triangles (total of 8)
5 binding strips, 2½" × 21" (for my chubby-binding method provided on page 126, reduce the strip width to 2")
Reserve the remainder of brown print #1.

From the 24 assorted print chubby sixteenths, cut a *combined total* of:
30 squares, 3½" × 3½"
Reserve the remainder of the 24 assorted print chubby sixteenths.

From the remainder of the 24 assorted print chubby sixteenths and brown print #1, cut a *combined total* of:
12 rectangles, 2" × 3½"
Reserve the scraps of the second brown print.

From the scraps of brown print #2, cut:
2 squares, 3⅞" × 3⅞"; cut each square in half diagonally *once* to yield 2 triangles (total of 4)

PIECING THE BLOCKS

*Sew all pieces with right sides together using a ¼"
seam allowance unless otherwise noted. Press the seam
allowances as indicated by the arrows or as otherwise
specified.*

1. Use a pencil and an acrylic ruler to draw a diagonal
sewing line from corner to corner on the wrong side of
the 72 assorted cream 1½" squares.

2. Layer a prepared cream 1½" square onto one
corner of a print 3½" square as shown. Stitch the pair
together along the drawn line. Fold the resulting inner
cream triangle open, aligning the corner with the
corner of the bottom square. Press. Trim away the
layers beneath the top triangle, leaving a ¼" seam
allowance. In the same manner, add a triangle to the
opposite corner of the square. Repeat to piece a total of
30 Patchwork blocks measuring 3½" square, including
seam allowances.

Make 30 Patchwork blocks,
3½" × 3½".

3. Choosing the prints randomly, join two of the
assorted print 2" × 3½" rectangles along the long edges.
Press. Repeat to piece a total of six pieced squares
measuring 3½" square, including seam allowances.

Make 6 pieced squares,
3½" × 3½".

4. Using the pieced squares from step 3 and the
remaining prepared cream 1½" squares, repeat step 2
to piece six Scrappy Variation blocks measuring 3½"
square, including seam allowances.

Make 6 Scrappy Variation blocks,
3½" × 3½".

PIECING THE QUILT CENTER

Lay out all the pieced blocks in six horizontal
rows of six blocks; the Scrappy Variation blocks can
be positioned as shown in the photo on page 57,
or you can create your own placement—the choice is

FINISHED QUILT SIZE: 18½" × 24½"   ◆   FINISHED BLOCK SIZE: 3" × 3"

Designed and pieced by Kim Diehl. Machine quilted by Rebecca Silbaugh.

2. Positioning the brown #1 and #2 prints randomly, lay out six half-square-triangle units. Join the units. Press. Repeat to piece a total of two border rows measuring 3½" × 18½", including seam allowances.

Make 2 border rows,
3½" × 18½".

3. Using the illustration as a guide, join the pieced border rows to the top and bottom edges of the quilt center. Press.

yours! Join the blocks in each row. Press. Join the rows. Press. The pieced quilt center should measure 18½" square, including the seam allowances.

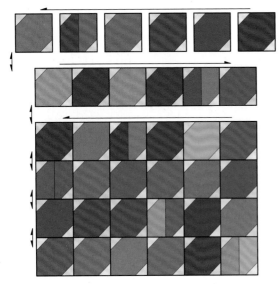

Quilt center assembly

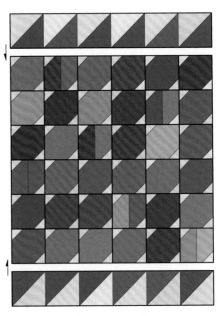

Adding the borders

ADDING THE BORDERS

1. Join a brown print #1 and a cream 3⅞" triangle along the long diagonal edges. Press. Trim away the dog-ear points. Repeat using the remaining brown print #1 and brown print #2 triangles, and the assorted cream triangles to piece a total of 12 half-square-triangle units measuring 3½" square, including the seam allowances.

Make 12 units,
3½" × 3½".

COMPLETING THE QUILT

Layer and baste the quilt top, batting, and backing. The featured quilt is machine quilted with a center diagonal line and gently curved surrounding lines in the whole blocks. The variation blocks are stitched with a gentle oval shape and filled in with repeating vertical lines. The brown sawtooth triangles are stitched with repeating V shapes and the cream sawtooth triangles with repeating vertical lines. Join the brown print #1 binding strips to make one length and use it to bind the quilt.

Windswept Pincushion

Raid your scrap basket and rescue the tiniest saved scraps of your favorite small-scale prints, and then stitch them up into this colorful patchwork pincushion. The wee checkerboard squares may look intimidating, but with one simple secret step, they become oh-so approachable.

FINISHED PATCHWORK:
5½" × 5½"
FINISHED PINCUSHION:
APPROXIMATELY 4" × 4"

Designed, pieced, and hand quilted in the
big-stitch style by Kim Diehl.

MATERIALS

*Yardage is based on a 42" width of useable fabric after
prewashing and removing selvages.*

+ 1 chubby sixteenth (9" × 10½") of black print for
  patchwork and backing

+ 6" × 6" square of cream print for patchwork

+ Assorted print scraps, equivalent to approximately
  one fat eighth (9" × 21"), for patchwork

+ 6" × 6" square of batting

+ #12 variegated perle cotton (I used Valdani's Ebony
  Almond, color O501)

+ Size 5 embroidery needle

+ Temporary adhesive basting spray for quilts
  (optional)

+ Crushed walnut shells to fill pincushion, or filling
  of your choice

CUTTING

*Cut all pieces across the width of the fabric in the order
given unless otherwise noted.*

From the black print, cut:
1 strip, 2¾" × 10½"; from this strip, cut:
    2 squares, 2¾" × 2¾"; cut each square in half
        diagonally *once* to yield 2 triangles (total of 4)
    3 squares, 1½" × 1½"
1 strip, 6" × 10½"; from this strip, cut:
    1 square, 6" × 6"
    1 square, 1½" × 1½" (combined total of 4 with
        previously cut squares)

From the cream print, cut:
1 strip, 2¾" × 6"; crosscut into 2 squares, 2¾" × 2¾".
    Cut each square in half diagonally *once* to yield
    2 triangles (total of 4).

From the assorted print scraps, cut:
4 squares (using a different print for each square),
    2⅜" × 2⅜"; cut each square in half diagonally *once*
    to yield 2 triangles (combined total of 8)
48 squares, 1¼" × 1¼" (For added choices when
    piecing the patchwork, you may wish to cut a
    handful of extra squares.)

PIECING THE DOUBLE-PINWHEEL UNIT

*Sew all pieces with right sides together using a ¼"
seam allowance unless otherwise noted. Press the seam
allowances as indicated by the arrows or as otherwise
specified.*

1. Layer together a black and a cream 2¾" triangle.
Stitch the pair along the long diagonal edge. Press.
Trim away the dog-ear points. Repeat to piece a total
of four black-and-cream half-square-triangle units
measuring 2⅜" square, including seam allowances.

Make 4 units,
2⅜" × 2⅜".

2. Select one 2⅜" triangle cut from a single assorted
print; layer and pin the triangle onto a black-and-cream
half-square-triangle unit as shown. Stitch the pair
together, ¼" in from the diagonal top triangle edge.
Press the triangle open. Trim away the bottom portion
of the black-and-cream half-square-triangle unit
leaving a ¼" seam allownace. Trim away the dog-ear
points. Discard the unused matching-print triangle.
Repeat to piece a total of four triple-triangle units
measuring 2" square, including seam allowances.

Make 4 units,
2" × 2".

3. Lay out the triple-triangle units in two horizontal
rows as shown. Join the units in each row. Press. Join
the rows. Press. The pieced double-pinwheel unit
should measure 3½" square, including seam allowances.

Make 1 Double-pinwheel unit,
3½" × 3½".

PIECING THE PINCUSHION

1. Choosing the prints randomly, select two assorted
print 1¼" squares. Join the squares. Press. Repeat to
piece a total of 24 two-patch units measuring 1¼" × 2",
including seam allowances.

Make 24 units,
1¼" × 2".

2. Lay out four two-patch units as shown, turning the
direction of one unit so the seams will nest together.
Join the units. Press. Repeat to piece a total of 12
four-patch units measuring 2" square, including seam
allowances.

Make 12 four-patch units,
2" × 2".

3. Here's my "secret" step to easily transform these
small-scale four-patch units to be even smaller. Using
a rotary cutter and an acrylic ruler, measure ¾" out
from the center vertical and horizontal four-patch
seams to trim the excess fabric on each side of the unit,

reducing the size to 1½" square, including seam allowances—this step will provide you with perfectly sized small-scale patchwork!

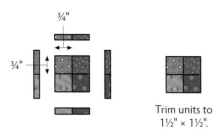

Trim units to
1½" × 1½".

4. Lay out the double-pinwheel unit and six four-patch units in two vertical rows as shown, rotating every other four-patch unit so the seams will nest together. Join the four-patch units in each row. Press. Join the pieced vertical four-patch rows to the right and left sides of the double-pinwheel unit. Press. The pieced unit should measure 3½" × 5½", including seam allowances.

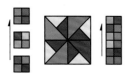

Make 1 unit,
3½" × 5½".

5. Lay out the remaining six four-patch units in two horizontal rows as shown, positioning the center unit in each row so the seams will nest with the seams of the double pinwheel unit. Join the four-patch rows. Press. Join a black 1½" square to each end of the four-patch rows. Press. Join these pieced rows to the top and bottom edges of the pincushion unit. Press. The pieced pincushion top should measure 5½" square, including seam allowances.

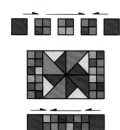 

Make 1 pincushion top,
5½" × 5½".

COMPLETING THE PINCUSHION UNIT

1. Layer the pincushion top onto the 6" square of batting (no backing fabric needed!), centering it. (Note: I applied temporary adhesive spray to the back of the pincushion top to help anchor it securely for the hand-stitching step, but this is entirely optional.) To keep the pincushion square and to prevent shifting as you hand stitch, I recommend stay-stitching around the perimeter of the unit, approximately ⅛" in from the raw edges.

2. Referring to "Big-Stitch Hand Quilting" on page 126, use the perle cotton and size 5 embroidery needle to hand quilt the pincushion. The featured pincushion was stitched ¼" out from selected seams in the double-pinwheel portion of the patchwork, the center double pinwheel unit is stitched in the ditch (along the seamlines), and Xs were stitched onto the four-patch units.

3. Trim away the excess batting. Layer the pincushion top with the black 6" backing square, centering it, and pin in place. Beginning near the center of one side edge and starting with a few back stitches or a locking stitch, sew the layers together around the perimeter of the patchwork using a ¼" seam allowance. Leaving a 1½" to 2" opening for turning, end with a few backstitches or a locking stitch.

4. At one corner of the pincushion, pull the front and back layers apart and smooth the unit flat with the corner point at the top, aligning the side seams so they rest in the center of the flattened unit. Using a pencil and an acrylic ruler, measure ¼" from the point of the corner seamline and draw a horizontal line, crossing through the aligned seams; pin the layers of the marked corner in place. Repeat to prepare the remaining corners of the pincushion. Stitch the pincushion corners on the drawn lines. Trim away the excess fabric at each stitched corner, leaving a

¼" seam allowance. This process will box the corners and produce a beautifully plump pincushion.

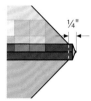

5. Turn the pincushion right side out and fill with crushed walnut shells (or filling of your choice). Use a needle and standard sewing thread in a neutral color to hand stitch the opening, taking tiny stitches to ensure no filling escapes.

✦ EXTRA SNIPPET ✦

Pastry Bag for the Win!

It can sometimes be a slow and messy process trying to spoon or pour crushed walnut shells into a pincushion, but if you happen to be a baker you may have just the right tool in your kitchen to make this step a snap—a pastry bag! Simply fit your bag with an open-style tip, add the walnut shells, and then watch them slide smoothly through the tip into your pincushion.

If you don't have a pastry bag, a quart-sized zippered plastic bag is the next best thing . . . just snip away one corner to create a funnel tip and you're in business!

This and That

What makes this petite sampler-style quilt so much fun to stitch? It's got to
be the "everything-but-the-kitchen-sink" approach to the block lineup,
making it possible to dabble in a pleasing and interesting mix of patchwork.
If variety is the spice of life, this mini is bringing all the flavors!

MATERIALS

*Yardage is based on a 42" width of useable fabric after
prewashing and removing selvages.*

- 19 chubby sixteenths (9" × 10½") of assorted prints
  for blocks and patchwork units
- 8 chubby sixteenths of assorted cream prints for
  blocks and patchwork units
- 1 fat quarter (18" × 21") of brown print for
  patchwork, border, and binding
- 1 fat quarter of teal print for patchwork and border
- ⅔ yard of fabric for backing
- 24" × 27" rectangle of batting
- Bias bar to make a ¼"-wide basket handle
- Water-soluble fabric glue
- Supplies for your favorite appliqué method

CUTTING FOR THE BORDER AND BINDING

*Cut all pieces across the width of the fabric in the order
given unless otherwise noted.*

From the brown print, cut:

4 strips, 1" × 21"
1 strip, 2⅞" × 21"; crosscut into 2 squares, 2⅞" × 2⅞".
  Cut each square in half diagonally *once* to yield
  2 triangles (total of 4). Trim the remainder of the
  strip to a 2½" width for use as binding.
4 additional binding strips, 2½" × 21" (for my
  chubby-binding method provided on page 126,
  reduce the strip width to 2")
Reserve the remainder of the brown print, including
  it with the assorted prints, for use in cutting the
  quilt-center patchwork pieces as needed.

From the teal print, cut:

4 strips, 2" × 21"
1 strip, 2⅞" × 21"; crosscut into 2 squares, 2⅞" × 2⅞".
  Cut each square in half diagonally *once* to yield
  2 triangles (total of 4). Reserve the remainder of
  the teal print, including it with the assorted prints,
  for use in cutting the quilt-center patchwork pieces
  as needed.

CUTTING AND PIECING THE BLOCKS AND PATCHWORK UNITS

*To simplify the cutting and piecing for the individual
components in this sampler design, these steps are
organized by the individual blocks so you can cut and piece
one section of the sampler at a time. Use the pictured quilt*

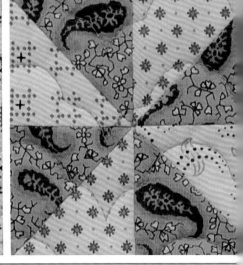

on page 64 for color choices, or choose your own mix of prints, cutting all pieces across the width of the fabric in the order given unless otherwise noted. When stitching the patchwork, sew all pieces with right sides together using a ¼" seam allowance unless otherwise noted. Press the seam allowances as indicated by the arrows or as otherwise specified.

2 Log Cabin Blocks

From the assorted prints, cut:
4 squares, 1½" × 1½"
4 rectangles, 1½" × 2½"
4 rectangles, 1½" × 3½"
4 rectangles, 1½" × 4½"
2 rectangles, 1½" × 5½"

Referring to the illustration, join two print 1½" squares. Press. Join a 1½" × 2½" rectangle to the pieced square unit as shown. Press. Continue sewing and pressing rectangles to the unit, working in a clockwise direction around the block and finishing with a 1½" × 5½" rectangle. Repeat to piece a total of two Log Cabin blocks measuring 5½" square, including seam allowances.

Make 2 Log Cabin blocks,
5½" × 5½".

1 Star Block

From the assorted cream prints, cut:
4 rectangles, 1½" × 2½"
4 squares, 1½" × 1½"

From 1 of the assorted prints (for the star points), cut:
8 squares, 1½" × 1½"

From a second of the assorted prints (for the star center), cut:
1 square, 2½" × 2½"

1. Use a pencil and an acrylic ruler to draw a diagonal sewing line from corner to corner on the wrong side of each star-point 1½" square. Layer a prepared square onto one end of a cream 1½" × 2½" rectangle. Fold the resulting inner triangle open, aligning the corner with the corner of the rectangle. Press. Trim away the layers beneath the top triangle, leaving a ¼" seam allowance. In the same manner, add a mirror-image triangle to the remaining end of the rectangle. Repeat to stitch a total of four star-point units measuring 1½" × 2½", including seam allowances.

Make 4 units,
1½" × 2½".

• 66 •

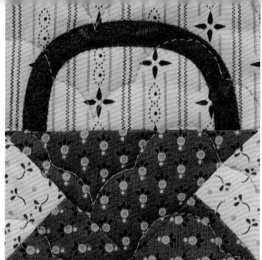

2. Referring to the illustration, lay out the four star-point units, the four cream 1½" squares, and the star center 2½" square in three horizontal rows. Join the pieces in each row. Press. Join the rows. Press. The pieced Star block should measure 4½" square, including seam allowances.

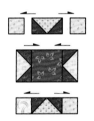

Make 1 Star block,
4½" × 4½".

2 Rail Fence Blocks

From the assorted cream prints, cut:
2 rectangles, 1½" × 3½"

From the assorted prints, cut:
4 rectangles, 1½" × 3½"

Join a print 1½" × 3½" rectangle to each long side of a cream 1½" × 3½" rectangle. Press. Repeat to piece a total of two Rail Fence blocks measuring 3½" square, including seam allowances.

Make 2 Rail Fence blocks,
3½" × 3½".

3 Square-in-a-Square Blocks

From the assorted cream prints, cut:
12 squares, 1½" × 1½"

From the assorted prints, cut:
3 squares, 2½" × 2½"

1. Prepare the 12 cream 1½" squares with a diagonal sewing line as previously instructed.

2. Referring to the Star block instructions, layer, stitch, press, and trim a prepared cream square onto two opposite corners of a print 2½" square. In the same manner, add cream triangles to the remaining corners of the square. Repeat to piece a total of three Square-in-a-Square blocks measuring 2½" square, including seam allowances.

Make 3 Square-in-a-Square blocks,
2½" × 2½".

1 Pinwheel Block

From the assorted cream prints, cut:
3 squares, 2⅜" × 2⅜"; cut each square in half diagonally *once* to yield 2 triangles (combined total of 6). Please note you'll use 2 triangles cut from one of the prints and 1 triangle cut from each of the 2 remaining prints, resulting in 2 unused cream triangles.

From 1 of the assorted prints, cut:
2 squares, 2⅜" × 2⅜"; cut each square in half diagonally *once* to yield 2 triangles (total of 4)

1. Join a print and a cream triangle along the long diagonal edges. Press. Trim away the dog-ear points. Repeat to piece a total of four half-square-triangle units measuring 2" square, including seam allowances.

Make 4 units,
2" × 2".

2. Lay out the half-square-triangle units in two horizontal rows as shown. Join the units in each row. Press. Join the rows. Press. The pieced Pinwheel block should measure 3½" square, including seam allowances.

Make 1 Pinwheel block,
3½" × 3½".

1 Basket Block

From 1 cream print, cut:
1 rectangle, 2" × 3½"

From a second cream print, cut;
1 square, 2⅜" × 2⅜"; cut the square in half diagonally *once* to yield 2 triangles

From 1 of the assorted prints (I chose chestnut), cut;
1 rectangle, 2" × 3½"
1 square, 2⅜" × 2⅜"; cut the square in half diagonally *once* to yield 2 triangles

From a second of the assorted prints (I chose brown), cut:
1 bias strip, 1" × 5½" (basket handle)

1. Using the cream and print triangles, refer to the Pinwheel block instructions above to layer, stitch, press, and trim away the dog-ear points for two half-square-triangle units measuring 2" square, including seam allowances. Draw a diagonal sewing line on the wrong side of the pieced units as shown.

2. Position a prepared half-square-triangle unit onto the print 2" × 3½" rectangle as shown. Stitch, press, and trim as previously instructed for the Star block on page 66 to add a pieced triangle to the rectangle. In the same manner, add a mirror-image pieced triangle to the remaining end of the rectangle to complete the basket base.

Make 1 unit,
2" × 3½".

3. With wrong sides together, fold the 1" × 5½" bias strip in half lengthwise; use a *scant* ¼" seam allowance to stitch along the long raw edges to form a tube. Trim the seam allowance to approximately ⅛". Use a bias bar to press the tube flat, centering the seam allowance so it will be hidden from the front.

4. After removing the bias bar, apply small dots of liquid fabric glue underneath the seam allowance; use a hot, dry iron to press the back of the tube and anchor the seam allowance in place. Referring to the illustration, use your favorite appliqué method to position, baste, and stitch the handle onto the cream 2" × 3½" rectangle. Trim the excess handle fabric even with the rectangle.

½" ½"

5. Join the appliquéd cream rectangle to the basket base from step 2 to complete one Basket block measuring 3½" square, including the seam allowances. Press.

Make 1 Basket block,
3½" × 3½".

12 Flying-Geese Units

From the assorted cream prints, cut:
24 squares, 1½" × 1½"

From the assorted prints, cut:
12 rectangles, 1½" × 2½"

Draw a diagonal sewing line on the wrong side of the 24 cream squares as previously instructed. Referring to the Star block instructions on page 66, use the prepared cream squares and the 12 assorted print rectangles to piece a total of 12 flying-geese units measuring 1½" × 2½", including seam allowances.

Make 12 units,
1½" × 2½".

1 Four-Patch Variation Block

From the assorted cream prints, cut:
2 squares, 2⅞" × 2⅞"; cut each square in half diagonally *once* to yield 2 triangles (combined total of 4). You'll use 1 triangle from each of these cream prints, resulting in 2 unused triangles.

From the assorted prints, cut:
2 squares, 2⅞" × 2⅞"; cut each square in half diagonally *once* to yield 2 triangles (combined total of 4). You'll use 1 triangle from each of these assorted prints, resulting in 2 unused triangles.
2 squares, 2½" × 2½" (Note: If you'd like to duplicate the prints used in my quilt and use the brown print for one square, you can easily cut them from one of the binding strips. You'll still have enough length to bind the quilt.)

1. Using the cream and assorted print triangles, refer to the Pinwheel block instructions on page 68 to layer, stitch, press, and trim away the dog-ear points for two half-square-triangle units measuring 2½" square, including seam allowances.

2. Lay out the two half-square-triangle units and the two assorted print 2½" squares in two horizontal rows as shown. Join the pieces in each row. Press. Join the

rows. Press. The pieced Four-Patch Variation block should measure 4½" square, including seam allowances.

Make 1 Four-Patch Variation block,
4½" × 4½".

1 Hourglass Block

From the assorted cream prints, cut:
2 squares, 4¼ × 4¼"; cut each square in half diagonally *twice* to yield 4 triangles (combined total of 8). You'll use 1 triangle from each of these 2 cream prints, resulting in 3 unused triangles from each print.

From the assorted prints, cut:
2 squares, 4¼ × 4¼"; cut each square in half diagonally *twice* to yield 4 triangles (combined total of 8). You'll use 1 triangle from each of these 2 assorted prints, resulting in 3 unused triangles from each print.

Join a cream and an assorted print triangle as shown. Press. Trim away the dog-ear points. Repeat to piece a total of two triangles. Join the pieced triangles as shown. Press. Trim away the dog-ear points. The pieced Hourglass block should measure 3½" square, including seam allowances.

Make 1 Hourglass block,
3½" × 3½".

1 Snowball Variation Block

From the assorted cream prints, cut:
4 squares, 1½'" × 1½"

From 1 of the assorted prints, cut:
2 rectangles, 1½" × 3½"
2 squares, 1½'" × 1½"

From a second of the assorted prints, cut:
1 square, 1½'" × 1½"

1. Draw a diagonal sewing line on the wrong side of the four cream squares as previously instructed. Referring to the Star block instructions on page 66, use the prepared cream squares and the print rectangles to piece a total of two snowball outer rows measuring 1½" × 3½", including seam allowances.

Make 2 snowball rows,
1½" × 3½".

2. Join and press the three assorted print 1½" squares as shown. Lay out this pieced center row with the two snowball outer rows as shown. Join the rows. Press. The pieced Snowball Variation block should measure 3½" square, including seam allowances.

Make 1 Snowball Variation block,
3½" × 3½".

5 Diagonal Stripe Units

From the assorted cream prints, cut:
10 squares, 1½" × 1½"

From the assorted prints, cut:
5 rectangles, 1½" × 3½"

Draw a diagonal sewing line on the wrong side of the 10 cream squares as previously instructed. Referring to the Star block instructions on page 66 and the illustration below, use the prepared cream squares and the five assorted print rectangles to piece a total of five diagonal stripe units measuring 1½" × 3½", including seam allowances.

Make 5 diagonal strip units,
1½" × 3½".

1 Nine Patch Block

From 1 cream print, cut:

3 squares, 1½" × 1½"

From a second cream print, cut:

1 square, 1½" × 1½"

From 1 of the assorted prints, cut:

4 squares, 1½" × 1½"

From a second print, cut:

1 square, 1½" × 1½"

Referring to the illustration, lay out the cream and print squares in three horizontal rows. Join the squares in each row. Press. Join the rows. Press. The pieced Nine Patch block should measure 3½" square, including seam allowances.

Make 1 Nine Patch block,
3½" × 3½".

5 Checkerboard Units

From 1 cream print, cut:

1 square, 1½" × 1½"

From the assorted prints, cut:

41 squares, 1½" × 1½"

1. Referring to the illustration, lay out 15 assorted print and one cream print 1½" squares in two horizontal rows. Join the squares in each row. Press. Join the rows. Press. Checkerboard unit A should measure 2½" × 8½", including seam allowances.

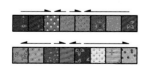

Make 1 checkerboard unit A,
2½" × 8½".

2. Using the illustration as a guide, lay out 12 assorted print 1½" squares in two horizontal rows. Join the squares in each row. Press. Join the rows. Press. Checkerboard unit B should measure 2½" × 6½", including seam allowances.

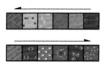
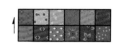

Make 1 checkerboard unit B,
2½" × 6½".

3. Referring to the illustration, lay out eight assorted print 1½" squares in two horizontal rows. Join the squares in each row. Press. Join the rows. Press. Checkerboard unit C should measure 2½" × 4½", including seam allowances.

Make 1 checkerboard unit C,
2½" × 4½".

4. Lay out and join three assorted print 1½" squares end to end. Press. Checkerboard unit D should measure 1½" × 3½", including seam allowances.

Make 1 checkerboard unit D,
1½" × 3½".

5. Lay out and join two assorted print 1½" squares. Press. Checkerboard unit E should measure 1½" × 2½", including seam allowances. Reserve the remaining assorted print 1½" square for later use.

Make 1 checkerboard unit E,
1½" × 2½".

FINISHED QUILT SIZE: 18½" × 21½"
FINISHED BLOCK SIZES: 5" × 5", 4" × 4", 3" × 3", AND 2" × 2"
Designed and pieced by Kim Diehl. Machine quilted by Connie Tabor.

Piecing the Sections for the Quilt Center

Please refer to the diagrams to piece the blocks and units indicated for each section.

1. For section 1, join and press:

   - 1 Log Cabin block
   - 1 Pinwheel block
   - 1 flying-geese unit
   - 1 reserved 1½" print square
   - Checkerboard unit E
   - 2 diagonal stripe units

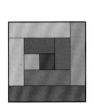

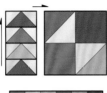

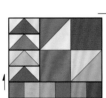

Section 1,
5½" × 9½"

2. For section 2, join and press:

   - 4 flying-geese units
   - 1 Four-Patch Variation block
   - Checkerboard unit B
   - 1 Nine Patch block
   - 3 diagonal stripe units

Section 2,
6½" × 9½"

3. For section 3, join and press:

   - 2 Rail Fence blocks
   - 3 Square-in-a-Square blocks
   - 1 Star block
   - Checkerboard unit C

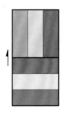

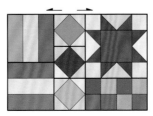

Section 3,
6½" × 9½"

4. For section 4, join and press:

   - 3 flying-geese units
   - 1 Snowball Variation block
   - Hourglass block
   - Checkerboard unit A

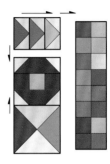

Section 4,
5½" × 8½"

5. For section 5, join and press:

   - Checkerboard unit D
   - 1 Basket block
   - 4 flying-geese units
   - 1 Log Cabin block

Section 5,
5½" × 9½"

ASSEMBLING THE QUILT CENTER

Using the assembly diagram as a guide, join and press the quilt-center patchwork sections. The pieced quilt center should measure 14½" × 17½", including seam allowances.

Quilt assembly

PIECING AND ADDING THE BORDER

1. Using the four brown and four teal 2⅞" triangles, refer to the Pinwheel block instructions on page 68 to layer, stitch, press seam allowances toward the brown print and trim away the dog-ear points to make four half-square-triangle units measuring 2½" square, including seam allowances.

2. Join a brown 1" × 21" strip to a teal 2" × 21" strip. Press the seam allowances toward the brown print. Repeat to piece a total of four strip sets measuring 2½" × 21", including seam allowances. From these pieced strip sets, cut two border units, 2½" × 14½", and two border units, 2½" × 17½".

3. Referring to the quilt photo on page 72, join a 2½" × 17½" border unit to the right and left side of the quilt center. Press the seam allowances toward the border. Join a half-square-triangle unit from step 1 to each end of the 2½" × 14½" border units. Press the seam allowances toward the border. Join these pieced units to the remaining sides of the quilt top. Press the seam allowances toward the border.

COMPLETING THE QUILT

Layer and baste the quilt top, batting, and backing. The featured quilt is machine quilted with an edge-to-edge pattern of repeating scalloped swags to unify the many different patchwork designs. Join the brown binding strips to make one length and use it to bind the quilt.

Twirligigs

Take a scrappy approach to the traditional Pinwheel block and what do you get? Sparkling "twirligigs" stitched from colorful checkerboard squares! This pieced table runner puts a planned spin on the color scheme, meaning that each print is used several times across the design for balance and continuity, resulting in a foolproof recipe for color success.

MATERIALS

Yardage is based on a 42" width of useable fabric after prewashing and removing selvages.

+ 17 chubby sixteenths (9" × 10½") of assorted prints for checkerboard
+ 4 chubby sixteenths of assorted cream prints for block triangles
+ ⅜ yard of black print for sashing strips and binding
+ ⅝ yard of fabric for backing
+ 21" × 37" rectangle of batting

CUTTING

Cut all pieces across the width of the fabric in the order given unless otherwise noted.

From *each* of the assorted prints, cut:
17 squares, 1½" × 1½" (combined total of 289)

From *each* of the 4 assorted cream prints, cut:
2 squares, 4⅞" × 4⅞" (combined total of 8); cut each square in half diagonally *once* to yield 2 triangles (combined total of 16)

From the black print, cut:
4 strips, 1" × 42"; from *each* of 2 strips, cut 1 strip, 1" × 24½" (total of 2), and 1 strip, 1" × 9½" (total of 2). From *each* of the remaining 2 strips, cut 1 strip, 1" × 27½" (total of 2), and 1 strip, 1" × 12½" (total of 2).
3 binding strips, 2½" × 42" (for my chubby-binding method provided on page 126, reduce the strip width to 2")

PIECING THE CHECKERBOARD AND PINWHEEL BLOCKS

Sew all pieces with right sides together using a ¼" seam allowance unless otherwise noted. Press the seam allowances as indicated by the arrows or as otherwise specified.

1. Choosing the prints randomly, lay out four 1½" squares end to end to form a row. Join the squares. Press. Repeat to piece a total of 12 checkerboard rows measuring 1½" × 4½", including the seam allowances.

Make 12 units,
1½" × 4½".

2. Repeat step 1, reducing the number of assorted print squares to three, to piece a total of 12 rows measuring 1½" × 3½", including seam allowances. Continue in this manner with two squares to piece a total of 12 rows measuring 1½" × 2½", including seam allowances.

Make 12 units,
1½" × 3½". Make 12 units,
1½" × 2½".

3. Lay out one pieced row in each size, from longest to shortest, alternating the direction of the pressed seam allowances in every other row so they'll nest together. Join the rows. Press. Join a single assorted print square to the two-square row as shown. Press. Repeat for a total of 12 pieced checkerboard triangle units. If needed, use a rotary cutter and acrylic ruler to square up the straight edge of each triangle unit so it's flush.

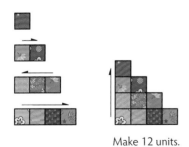

Make 12 units.

4. Layer a cream 4⅞" triangle onto a checkerboard unit, aligning the corners and straight edges; pin the cream triangle in place along the diagonal edge. Stitch the pair together along the cream diagonal edge using a ¼" seam allowance. Trim away the excess portions of the checkerboard squares that extend beyond the

cream triangle, leaving the ¼" seam allowance intact. Press. Repeat to piece a total of 12 half-square-triangle checkerboard units measuring 4½" square, including seam allowances. Please note you'll have four unused cream triangles.

Make 12 units,
4½" × 4½".

5. Lay out four pieced half-square-triangle checkerboard units in two horizontal rows as shown. Join the units in each row. Press. Join the rows. Press. Repeat to piece a total of three Checkerboard Pinwheel blocks measuring 8½" square, including seam allowances.

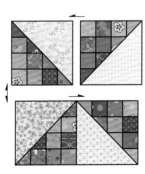

Make 3 blocks,
8½" × 8½".

FINISHED QUILT SIZE: 14½" × 30½" ◆ **FINISHED BLOCK SIZE: 8" × 8"**

Designed and pieced by Kim Diehl. Machine quilted by Lois Walker.

PIECING THE QUILT CENTER

Using the pictured quilt on page 78 as a guide, join the Checkerboard Pinwheel blocks end to end. Press the seam allowances open. The pieced quilt center should measure 8½" × 24½", including seam allowances.

PIECING AND ADDING THE BORDERS AND SASHING STRIPS

Please refer to the quilt-center assembly diagram at right as a guide for the steps that follow.

1. Join a black print 1" × 24½" strip to each long side of the quilt center. Press. Join a black print 1" × 9½" strip to each remaining side of the quilt center. Press.

2. Choosing the prints randomly, join 25 assorted 1½" squares end to end. Press. Repeat to piece a total of two checkerboard strips measuring 1½" × 25½" including seam allowances. Join these checkerboard strips to each long side of the quilt top. Press. In the same manner, join 11 assorted print 1½" squares. Press. Repeat to piece a total of two pieced checkerboard strips measuring 1½" × 11½", including seam allowances. Join these strips to the remaining sides of the quilt top, turning the direction of one strip so the pressed seam allowances of the end checkerboard square will nest with the seam of the black border strip. The quilt top should measure 11½" × 27½", including seam allowances.

Make 2 side borders, 1½" × 25½".

Make 2 inner top/bottom borders, 1½" × 11½".

3. Join a black 1" × 27½" strip to each long side of the quilt top. Press. Join a black 1" × 12½" strip to each remaining side of the quilt top. Press.

4. Choosing the prints randomly, join 28 assorted print 1½" squares end to end. Press the seam allowances in one direction. Repeat to piece a total of two checkerboard strips measuring 1½" × 28½", including

seam allowances. Join these strips to each long side of the quilt top. Press. In the same manner, join 14 assorted 1½" squares. Press the seam allowances in one direction. Repeat to piece a total of two checkerboard strips measuring 1½" × 14½". Join these strips to the remaining sides of the quilt top, turning the direction of one strip so the pressed seam allowances of the end checkerboard square will nest with the seam of the black border strip. You'll have 13 unused print squares. These have been included for added choices as you stitch the patchwork.

Quilt assembly

COMPLETING THE QUILT

Layer and baste the quilt top, batting, and backing. Quilt the layers. The featured quilt is machine quilted with an X stitched onto each checkerboard square. The Checkerboard Pinwheel blocks are stitched in the ditch (along the seamline) of each diagonal seam. Feathered wreath halves are stitched onto the cream triangle areas. The black sashing strips are stitched in the ditch. Join the black binding strips to make one length and use it to bind the quilt.

Village Square

Inspired by my love of vintage game boards, this pieced and appliquéd quilt takes the tried-and-true Churn Dash block and elevates it to a whole new level. Strip-pieced setting blocks ramp up your patchwork speed, and the surrounding vines blooming with gently shaped berries, buds, and birds provide the sweet icing on the quilt cake.

MATERIALS

Yardage is based on a 42" width of usable fabric after prewashing and removing selvages.

- ¼ yard (not a fat quarter) of gold print for strip-set units
- ¼ yard (not a fat quarter) of cream print #1 for strip-set units and framed squares
- ¼ yard (not a fat quarter) of red print for strip-set units and appliqués
- ⅝ yard of dark blue print for framed squares, sashing square, inner border, and binding
- 6 chubby sixteenths (9" × 10½") of assorted prints for churn dash units and appliqués
- 1 fat eighth (9" × 21") *each* of bright green and medium blue prints for churn dash units and appliqués
- 1 fat quarter (18" × 21") of cream print #2 for churn dash units
- 1 chubby sixteenth of cream print #3 for churn dash units
- ½ yard of brown print for sashing strips and outer border
- ⅔ yard of cream stripe for appliqué border
- ⅓ yard of dark green print for vines and appliqués
- 1 fat eighth of green print for appliqués
- 4 chubby sixteenths of assorted prints (including black) for appliqués
- 1¼ yards of fabric for backing
- 44" × 44" square of batting

- Bias bar to make ⅜"-wide stems
- Water-soluble fabric glue
- Freezer paper for making vine placement guide
- Water-soluble marker
- Supplies for your favorite appliqué method

CUTTING

Cut all pieces across the width of the fabric in the order given unless otherwise noted. For greater ease, cutting instructions for the appliqués are provided separately.

From the gold print, cut:
4 strips, 1" × 42"

From cream print #1, cut:
4 strips, 1" × 42"
4 squares, 2½" × 2½"

From the red print, cut:
2 strips, 1½" × 42"
Reserve the scraps for the appliqués.

From the dark blue print, cut:
2 strips, 1" × 42"; crosscut into:
    8 rectangles, 1" × 2½"
    8 rectangles, 1" × 3½"
7 strips, 2½" × 42"; crosscut into:
    2 strips, 2½" × 20½"
    2 strips, 2½" × 24½"
    1 square, 2½" × 2½"
Reserve the remainder of the 2½"-wide strips for the binding (for my chubby-binding method provided on page 126, reduce the strip width to 2").

Continued on page 82

Continued from page 81

From *each* of the 6 assorted print chubby sixteenths and the bright green and medium blue print fat eighths designated for the churn dash units, cut:

4 squares, 1⅞" × 1⅞" (combined total of 32); cut each square in half diagonally *once* to yield 2 triangles (combined total of 64)

2 strips, 1" × approximately 10½" (combined total of 16)

Keep the pieces organized by print and reserve the scraps for the appliqués.

From the cream #2 print, cut:

8 strips, 1" × 21"; cut each strip in half to make a total of 16 strips, 1" × approximately 10½"

32 squares, 1⅞" × 1⅞"; cut each square in half diagonally *once* to yield a total of 64 triangles

From cream print #3, cut:

16 squares, 1½" × 1½"

From the brown print, cut:

1 strip, 2½" × 42"; crosscut into 4 strips, 2½" × 9½"

2 strips, 2½" × 33½"

2 strips, 2½" × 37½"

From the cream stripe, cut:

2 strips, 5" × 24½"

2 strips, 5" × 33½"

From the dark green print, cut:

Enough 1¼"-wide *bias* strips to make two 30" lengths and two 40" lengths when joined end to end.

Reserve the scraps for the appliqués.

Piecing the Strip-Set Units

Sew all pieces with right sides together using a ¼" seam allowance unless otherwise noted. Press the seam allowances as indicated by the arrows or as otherwise specified.

1. Join a cream 1" × 42" strip to each long edge of a red 1½" × 42" strip. Sew a gold 1" × 42" strip to each of the cream strips to make a strip set measuring 3½" × 42", including seam allowances. Press. Repeat to piece a total of two strip sets.

2. Crosscut the pieced strip sets at 3½" intervals to make 16 strip-set units measuring 3½" × 3½", including seam allowances.

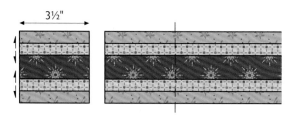

Make 2 strip sets, 3½" × 42".
Cut 16 units, 3½" × 3½".

Piecing the Framed-Square Units

1. Join a dark blue 1" × 2½" rectangle to opposite sides of a 2½" cream print #1 square. Press. Repeat to piece a total of four center block segments measuring 2½" × 3½", including seam allowances.

2. Join a dark blue 1" × 3½" rectangle to the remaining edges of a center block segment. Press. Repeat to piece a total of four framed-square units measuring 3½" square, including seam allowances.

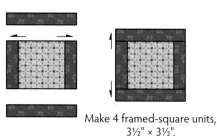

Make 4 framed-square units,
3½" × 3½".

Piecing the Churn-Dash Units

1. From the assorted prints, select two matching print 1" × 10½" strips and four matching print 1⅞" squares, for a churn unit. Join a cream print #2 and a print 1" × 10½" strip along the long edges to make a strip set. Repeat to piece a total of two strip sets. Crosscut the strip sets at 1½" intervals to make eight pieced block segments.

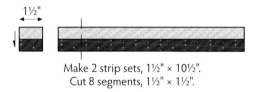

Make 2 strip sets, 1½" × 10½".
Cut 8 segments, 1½" × 1½".

2. Join a print and a cream print #2 triangle along the long diagonal edges. Press. Trim away the dog-ear points. Repeat to piece a total of eight half-square-triangle units measuring 1½" square, including seam allowances.

Make 8 units,
1½" × 1½".

3. Lay out four block segments, four half-square-triangle units from step 2, and one 1½" cream print #3 square as shown. Join the pieces in each horizontal row. Press. Join the rows. Press. Repeat to piece a total of two churn-dash units measuring 3½" square, including seam allowances.

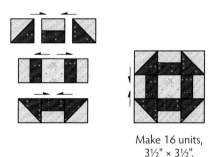

Make 16 units,
3½" × 3½".

4. Repeat to piece a total of 16 churn-dash units measuring 3½" square, with two units stitched from each of the eight prints called for.

PIECING THE BLOCKS

Lay out four strip-set units, one framed-square unit, and four churn-dash units as shown. Join the pieces in each horizontal row. Press. Join the rows. Press. Repeat to piece a total of four blocks measuring 9½" square, including seam allowances.

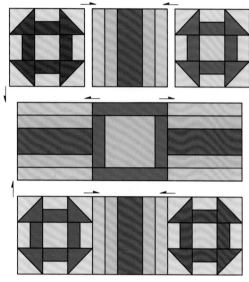

Make 4 blocks,
9½" × 9½".

PIECING THE QUILT CENTER

1. Referring to the photo on page 85 and the assembly diagram on page 87, join a pieced block to opposite long sides of a brown print 2½" × 9½" sashing strip. Press the seam allowances toward the sashing. Repeat to make a total of two block rows.

2. Join a brown print 2½" × 9½" sashing strip to opposite sides of the dark blue print 2½" square to make a sashing row. Press the seam allowances toward the sashing strips.

3. Again referring to the photo, lay out the block rows from step 1 and the sashing row from step 2 to form the quilt center. Join the rows. Press the seam allowances toward the sashing row. The quilt center should measure 20½" square, including seam allowances.

APPLIQUÉING THE MIDDLE BORDER

Step-by-step instructions for my invisible machine-appliqué method begin on page 121, or you can use your own favorite method. Appliqué patterns are provided on page 88.

1. Trace the vine curve guide provided on page 88 onto the dull, nonwaxy side of a 4" × 10" piece of freezer paper. Layer a second piece of freezer paper under the traced piece. With waxy sides together and use a hot, dry iron to fuse the layers. Cut out the guide exactly along the drawn lines. Fold the guide in half, aligning the ends, and finger-press a center vertical crease.

2. Fold a cream stripe border strip in half widthwise and use a hot, dry iron to lightly press a center crease. Repeat to crease all four cream strips.

3. Line up the center crease of the vine guide with the center crease of a cream strip, keeping the bottom edge of the guide flush with the bottom edge of the strip. Use a water-soluble marker to trace the curved line onto the strip, working from the center of the strip out toward each end. Repeat for four marked strips.

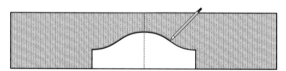

4. Join the dark green 1¼"-wide bias strips end to end to make two strips 30" in length and two strips 40" in length. Press the seam allowances to one side (not open), all in the same direction.

5. Referring to "Making Bias-Tube Stems and Vines" on page 124, prepare the vines. After removing the bias bar, apply small dots of liquid fabric glue underneath the pressed seam allowance of each vine at approximately ½" intervals. Use a hot, dry iron to heat set the glue and anchor the seams in place.

Village Square

Finished quilt size: 37½" × 37½" ✦ **Finished block size: 9" × 9"**

Designed, pieced, and appliquéd by Kim Diehl. Machine quilted by Deborah Poole.

6. Dot the traced vine curve on a cream stripe 24½"-long strip from step 3 with liquid glue at approximately ½" intervals. Lay out a prepared 30" vine along the traced curve, centering it over the drawn line and pushing it firmly in place onto the strip with your hand. From the back of the strip, heat set the vine with a hot iron. Repeat to make a second 24½"-long strip. In the same manner, glue baste the 40" prepared vines to each of the cream stripe 33½"-long strips.

7. Using the reserved assorted print scraps and referring to the pictured quilt on page 85 as you make your color choices, cut and prepare the following appliqués:

- 4 birds
- 4 bird wings
- 12 blossoms
- 12 blossom bases
- 36 leaves
- 30 berries

8. Using a prepared 24½"-long strip from step 6 and referring to the pictured quilt, work from the bottom layer to the top to lay out and stitch one bird and bird wing, two blossoms and blossom bases, eight leaves, and seven berries. Ensure that any overlapping pieces do so by at least ¼". Trim away any excess vine length at each end of the appliquéd border strip. Repeat to appliqué a second 24½" strip.

9. Repeat step 8 using the prepared 33½"-long strips, stitching one bird and bird wing, four blossoms and blossom bases, 10 leaves, and eight berries to each.

ADDING THE BORDERS TO THE QUILT TOP

1. Join a dark blue print 2½" × 20½" strip to the right and left sides of the quilt center. Press. Stitch a dark blue 2½" × 24½" strip to each remaining side of the quilt center. Press.

2. Join an appliquéd 24½" strip to the right and left sides of the quilt top. Press. Stitch an appliquéd 33½" strip to each remaining side of the quilt top. Press.

3. Join a brown 2½" × 33½" strip to the right and left sides of the quilt top. Press. Stitch a brown 2½" × 37½" strip to each remaining side of the quilt top. Press.

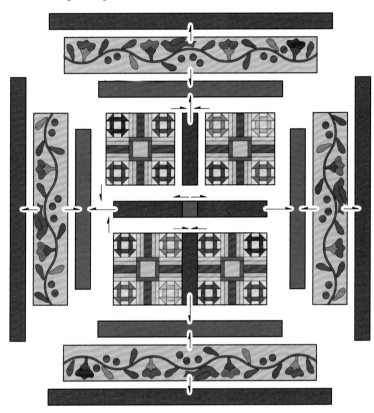

Quilt assembly

COMPLETING THE QUILT

Layer the quilt top, batting, and backing. Quilt the layers. The featured quilt is machine quilted in the ditch (along the seamlines) of the churn-dash units and strip-set units, with the stitched lines of the strip-set units crossing over the block-center squares. The sashing strips and center sashing square are stitched with Xs. The appliqués are outlined to emphasize their shapes and straight lines are stitched onto the middle border background areas using the stripe pattern as a guide. Join the remaining dark blue strips to make one length and use it to bind the quilt.

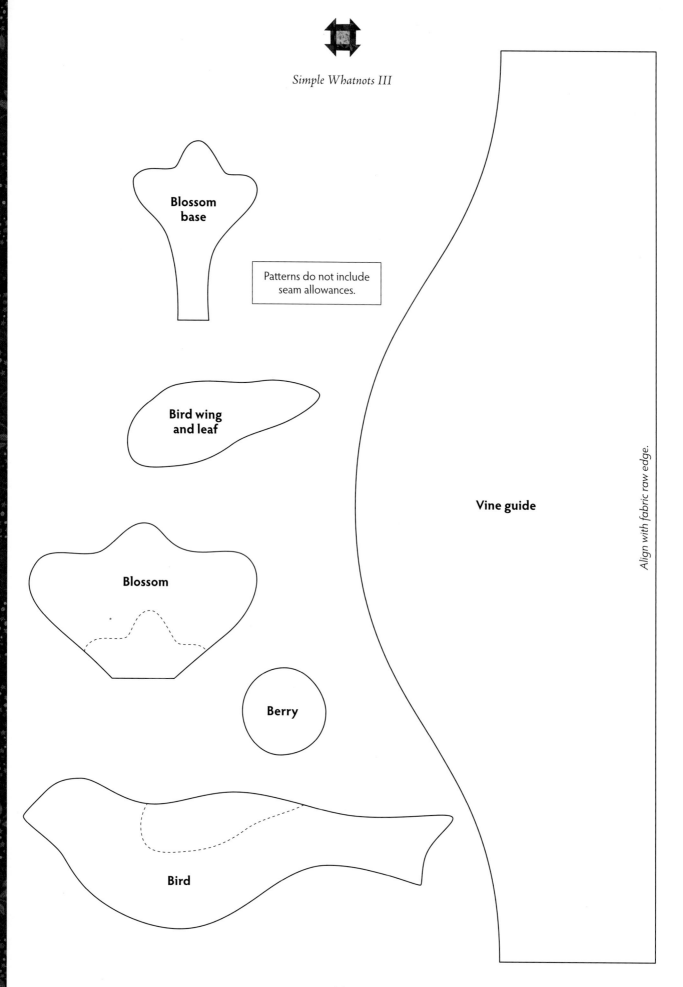

Blossom base

Patterns do not include seam allowances.

Bird wing and leaf

Vine guide

Align with fabric raw edge.

Blossom

Berry

Bird

Ribbon Candy

As a kid, I saw ribbon candy for the first time and thought it had to be one of the prettiest and yummiest holiday treats ever. Inspired by that memory, this pieced mini is incredibly easy to stitch, just the right size to tuck into any small nook, and just as pretty and yummy as the sweet treats I remember.

MATERIALS

Yardage is based on a 42" width of useable fabric after prewashing and removing selvages.

- 1 fat eighth (9" × 21") *each of dark red, medium red, and medium green prints for patchwork*
- ⅜ yard of dark green print for patchwork and binding
- 1 fat quarter (18" × 21") *each of cream print #1 and cream print #2 for patchwork*
- ⅔ yard of fabric for backing
- 24" × 24" square of batting

CUTTING

Cut all pieces across the width of the fabric in the order given unless otherwise noted.

From the dark red print, cut:
3 strips, 1¼" × 21"
1 strip, 2¾" × 21"; crosscut into 4 squares, 2¾" × 2¾"

From *each* of the medium red and medium green prints, cut:
3 strips, 1¼" × 21" (combined total of 6)
1 strip, 2¾" × 21"; crosscut into 4 rectangles, 2¾" × 5"
   (combined total of 8)

From the dark green print, cut:
2 strips, 1¼" × 42"; crosscut into 3 strips, 1¼" × 21"
1 strip, 2¾" × 42"; crosscut into 4 rectangles, 2¾" × 5".
   From the remainder of this strip, cut one length of
   binding, 2½" × 21" (see note below).
2 additional binding strips, 2½" × 42" (For my
   chubby-binding method provided on page 126,
   reduce the strip width to 2".)

From cream #1, cut:
3 strips, 1¼" × 21"
2 strips, 2¾" × 21"; crosscut into 8 squares, 2¾" × 2¾"

From cream #2, cut:
3 strips, 1¼" × 21"
3 strips, 2¾" × 21"; crosscut into 16 squares,
   2¾" × 2¾"

PIECING THE RAIL FENCE UNITS

Sew all pieces with right sides together using a ¼" seam allowance unless otherwise noted. Press the seam allowances as indicated by the arrows or as otherwise specified.

1. Join a dark and a medium red strip to each long side of a cream #1 strip. Press. Repeat to piece three strip sets measuring 2¾" × 21", including seam allowances.

2. Cut the strip sets at 2¾" intervals to make 20 red strip-set units, 2¾" × 2¾".

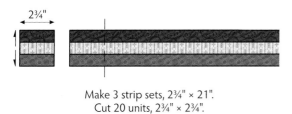

Make 3 strip sets, 2¾" × 21".
Cut 20 units, 2¾" × 2¾".

3. Using the dark green, medium green, and cream #2 strips, repeat steps 1 and 2 to piece 16 green strip-set units, 2¾" × 2¾".

PIECING THE RIBBON BLOCKS

1. Lay out four red strip-set units in two horizontal rows as shown. Join the segments in each row. Press. Join the rows. Press. Repeat to piece a total of five red Ribbon blocks measuring 5" square, including the seam allowances.

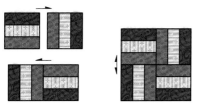

Make 5 red Ribbon blocks,
5" × 5".

2. Using the green strip-set segments, repeat step 1 to piece a total of four green Ribbon blocks measuring 5" square, including the seam allowances.

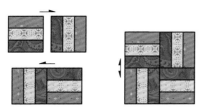

Make 4 green Ribbon blocks,
5" × 5".

PIECING THE QUILT CENTER

Referring to the illustration, lay out the red and green Ribbon blocks in three horizontal rows. Join the blocks in each row. Press. Join the rows. Press.

The quilt center should measure 14" square, including the seam allowances.

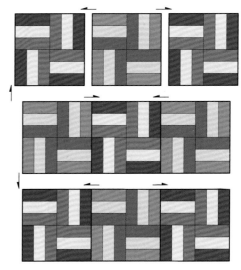

Quilt center assembly

PIECING AND ADDING THE FLYING-GEESE BORDER

1. Use a pencil and an acrylic ruler to draw a diagonal sewing line from corner to corner on the wrong side of each 2¾" cream #1 and cream #2 square.

2. Select a dark green 2¾" × 5" rectangle and two prepared cream #2 squares. Layer a prepared cream square onto one end of the green rectangle as shown. Stitch the pair together along the drawn line. Fold the resulting inner cream triangle open, aligning the corner with the corner of the green rectangle. Press. Trim away the layers beneath the top triangle, leaving a ¼" seam allowance. In the same manner, add a mirror-image triangle point to the remaining end of the green rectangle. Repeat to piece four dark green flying-geese units measuring 2¾" × 5", including the seam allowances.

Make 4 dark green units,
2¾" × 5".

FINISHED QUILT SIZE: 18½" × 18½" ✦ **FINISHED BLOCK SIZE: 4½" × 4½"**
Designed and pieced by Kim Diehl. Machine quilted by Connie Tabor.

3. Using the medium red 2¾" × 5" rectangles and the prepared 2¾" cream #1 squares, as well as the medium green 2¾" × 5" rectangles and the prepared 2¾" cream #2 squares, repeat step 2 to piece four medium red units and four medium green flying-geese units measuring 2¾" × 5", including the seam allowances.

Make 4 of each unit,
2¾" × 5".

4. Lay out one each of the dark green, medium red, and medium green flying-geese units as shown. Join the units. Press. Repeat to piece a total of four flying-geese border strips measuring 2¾" × 14", including the seam allowances.

Make 4 border strips,
2¾" × 14".

5. Referring to the illustration, join a flying-geese border strip to the right and left sides of the quilt center. Press. Join a dark red 2¾" square to each end of the remaining flying-geese border strips. Press. Join

these completed strips to the top and bottom edges of the quilt center. Press.

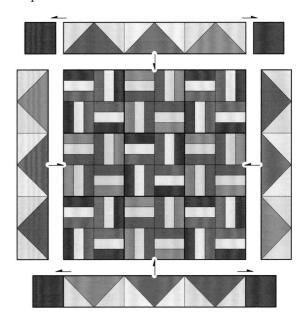

Adding the borders

COMPLETING THE QUILT

Layer and baste the quilt top, batting, and backing. Quilt the layers. The featured quilt is quilted with an edge-to-edge design of meandering feathered clusters. Join the dark green binding strips to make one length and use it to bind the quilt.

Cross Purposes

While treating myself to a little guilty-pleasure TV time one day, I realized that I was also in the mood for some autopilot stitching—meaning something totally uncomplicated that would come together quickly. With no seams to be matched, this sweet mini ticked all my wish-list boxes, plus it was a perfect stash buster!

MATERIALS

Yardage is based on a 42" width of useable fabric after prewashing and removing selvages.

- Approximately ¼ yard of assorted dark and medium print scraps (referred to collectively as "dark") for patchwork
- Approximately ¼ yard of assorted cream print scraps (referred to collectively as "light") for patchwork
- 1 fat eighth (9" × 21") of dark brown print for binding
- 1 fat quarter of fabric for backing
- 19" × 22" rectangle of batting

CUTTING

Cut all pieces across the width of the fabric in the order given unless otherwise noted. You may wish to cut an extra handful of the dark and light rectangles for added choices as you stitch the patchwork.

From the dark scraps, cut:
53 rectangles, 1½" × 2½"

From the light scraps, cut:
44 rectangles, 1½" × 2½"

From the dark brown print, cut:
3 binding strips, 2½" × 21" (for my chubby-binding method on page 126, reduce the strip width to 2")

PIECING THE QUILT ROWS

Sew all pieces with right sides together using a ¼" seam allowance unless otherwise noted. Press the seam allowances as indicated by the arrows or as otherwise specified.

1. Referring to the illustration, lay out four dark and two light 1½" × 2½" rectangles. Join the rectangles. Press. Repeat to piece a total of six A rows measuring 1½" × 12½", including the seam allowances.

Make 6 A rows,
1½" × 12½".

2. Using the illustration as a guide, lay out three dark and four light 1½" × 2½" rectangles. Join the rectangles. Press. Repeat to piece a total of three B rows measuring 1½" × 14½", including the seam allowances.

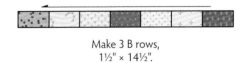

Make 3 B rows,
1½" × 14½".

3. Referring to the illustration, lay out four dark and three light 1½" × 2½" rectangles. Join the rectangles. Press. Repeat to piece a total of four C rows measuring 1½" × 14½", including the seam allowances.

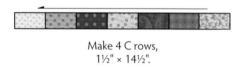

Make 4 C rows,
1½" × 14½".

4. Lay out two dark and four light 1½" × 2½" rectangles as shown. Join the rectangles. Press. Repeat to piece a total of two D rows measuring 1½" × 12½", including the seam allowances.

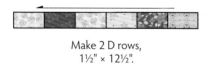

Make 2 D rows,
1½" × 12½".

PIECING THE QUILT TOP

1. Using the quilt assembly diagram as a guide, lay out and join the quilt rows. (Note: Since there are no seams to be matched, you can estimate the placement of the 14½"-long rows, with the excess length distributed evenly at each end. Or, to be more precise in your placement, you can do as I did and fold each row in half, finger-press the center position, and line up this center crease with the center seam of the row it will rest next to—this step will produce perfectly centered patchwork rows!)

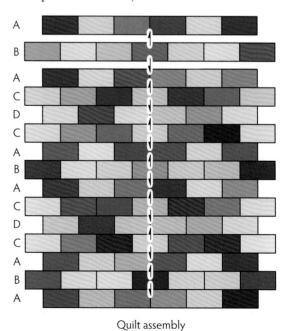

Quilt assembly

Cross Purposes

FINISHED QUILT SIZE: 12½" × 15½"

Designed and pieced by Kim Diehl. Machine quilted by Connie Tabor.

2. Use a rotary cutter and an acrylic ruler to trim the excess length from each long row. The quilt top should measure 12½" × 15½", including seam allowances.

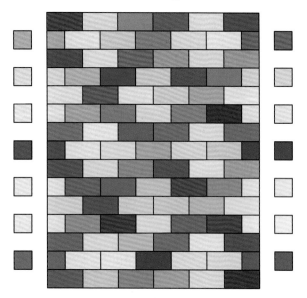

Trim quilt top to
12½" × 15½".

COMPLETING THE QUILT

Layer and baste the quilt top, batting, and backing. Quilt the layers. The featured quilt is machine quilted with rows of connected loops that alternate upward and downward, with the rows staggered to produce even texture across the quilt top. Join the dark brown print strips to make one length and use it to bind the quilt.

Alternate Possibilities

In addition to being a quick-and-easy patchwork mini to stitch, the dark and light rectangles in this design can be shuffled and rearranged to provide a variety of different looks. Honestly, the possibilities are endless, but here are two quick variations to inspire your creativity. For the completely scrappy darker version, you'll need 97 dark 1½" × 2½" rectangles. For the second look shown, you'll need 44 dark and 53 light 1½" × 2½" rectangles. Using the pictured examples as a guide for color placement, follow the pattern of the short and long row positions as instructed for the featured quilt, trim the side edges, and you're in business!

Alternate colorways

Midnight

Create your own little universe as you stitch a sprinkling of stars from a soothing palette of teal, aqua, and taupey gray. Notice how the gray stars seem to peek out from behind the large center star? Strategic yet simple piecing makes this illusion a snap to achieve—no need to fess up about this, just smile, drink in the compliments, and enjoy your quilt!

MATERIALS

Yardage is based on a 42" width of useable fabric after prewashing and removing selvages.

- 1 fat quarter (18" × 21") of turquoise print for quilt-center patchwork
- 1 chubby sixteenth (9" × 10½") of blue print for quilt-center patchwork
- ½ yard of teal print for quilt-center patchwork, border, and binding
- 1 fat quarter of cream print for quilt-center patchwork
- 1 fat quarter of gray print for quilt-center patchwork and border
- 1 fat quarter of aqua print for border
- ¾ yard of fabric for backing
- 27" × 27" square of batting

CUTTING

Cut all pieces across the width of the fabric in the order given unless otherwise noted.

From the turquoise print, cut:
2 strips, 2½" × 21"; crosscut into 12 squares, 2½" × 2½"
4 strips, 1½" × 21"; crosscut into 48 squares, 1½" × 1½"

From the blue print, refer to the cutting diagram below to cut:
1 square, 4½" × 4½"
8 squares, 2½" × 2½"

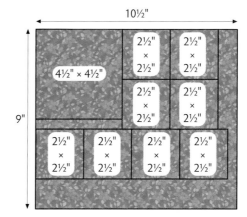

Blue print cutting diagram

Continued on page 101

Continued from page 99

From the teal print, cut:

3 strips, 2½" × 42". Crosscut *1 strip* into 12 squares, 2½" × 2½"; reserve the remainder of this strip, as well as the additional 2 strips, for the binding. (For my chubby-binding method provided on page 126, reduce the strip width to 2".)

1 additional strip, 2½" × 42"; crosscut into:
  8 squares, 2½" × 2½" (combined total of 20 with previously cut squares)
  4 rectangles, 2½" × 4½"

1 strip, 4½" × 42"; crosscut into 8 squares, 4½" × 4½"

From the cream print, cut:

7 strips, 1½" × 21"; crosscut into:
  32 rectangles, 1½" × 2½"
  32 squares, 1½" × 1½"

2 strips, 2½" × 21"; crosscut into 8 rectangles, 2½" × 4½"

From the gray print, cut:

4 strips, 1½" × 21"; crosscut into 48 squares, 1½" × 1½"

3 strips, 2½" × 21"; crosscut into 20 squares, 2½" × 2½"

From the aqua print, cut:

4 strips, 2½" × 21"; crosscut into 16 rectangles, 2½" × 4½"

PIECING THE CENTER STAR BLOCK

Sew all pieces with right sides together using a ¼" seam allowance unless otherwise noted. Press the seam allowances as indicated by the arrows or as otherwise specified.

1. Use a pencil and an acrylic ruler to draw a diagonal sewing line from corner to corner on the wrong side of the 12 turquoise 2½" squares.

2. Layer a prepared turquoise 2½" square onto two opposite corners of the blue 4½" square as shown, above right. Stitch the small squares to the large square along the drawn lines. Fold the resulting inner triangles open, aligning the corners with the corners of the bottom square. Press. Trim away the layers beneath the top triangles, leaving ¼" seam allowances. In the same manner, add turquoise triangles to the remaining corners of the blue square. The pieced square-in-a-square unit should measure 4½" square, including the seam allowances. Reserve the remaining prepared 2½" turquoise squares for step 3.

Make 1 unit,
4½" × 4½".

3. Layer a reserved prepared turquoise 2½" square onto one end of a teal 2½" × 4½" rectangle as shown. Stitch, press, and trim as previously instructed. In the same manner, add a turquoise mirror-image triangle to the remaining end of the teal rectangle. Repeat to piece a total of four turquoise star-point units measuring 2½" × 4½", including the seam allowances.

Make 4 units,
2½" × 4½".

4. Lay out the step 2 square-in-a-square unit, the four turquoise star-point units, and four teal 2½" squares in three horizontal rows as shown. Join the pieces in each row. Press. Join the rows. Press. The center Star block should measure 8½" square, including the seam allowances. Reserve the 16 remaining teal 2½" squares for use in the border.

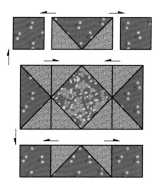

Make 1 center Star block,
8½" × 8½".

PIECING THE QUILT CENTER

1. Draw a diagonal sewing line on the wrong side of each of the 48 gray and 48 turquoise 1½" squares as previously instructed.

2. Using one blue 2½" square and 4 prepared gray 1½" squares per unit, follow step 2 of "Piecing the Center Star Block" on page 101 to piece four gray square-in-a-square units measuring 2½" square, including the seam allowances. In the same manner, use the remaining blue 2½" squares and the prepared turquoise 1½" squares to piece four turquoise square-in-a-square units measuring 2½" square, including the seam allowances.

Make 4 of each unit,
2½" × 2½".

3. Using eight prepared gray 1½" squares, four cream 1½" × 2½" rectangles, and four cream 1½" squares per block, follow steps 3 and 4 of "Piecing the Center Star Block" on page 101 to piece four gray small Star blocks measuring 4½" square, including the seam allowances. In the same manner, use the prepared turquoise squares, cream 1½" × 2½" rectangles, and cream 1½" squares to piece four turquoise small Star blocks measuring 4½" square, including the seam allowances.

Make 4 of each small Star block,
4½" × 4½".

4. Select one gray small Star block and two cream 2½" × 4½" rectangles. Join the cream rectangles to the right and left sides of the block. Press. Repeat to piece a total of four gray star units measuring 4½" × 8½", including the seam allowances.

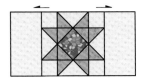

Make 4 gray star units,
4½" × 8½".

Midnight

FINISHED QUILT SIZE: 20½" × 20½"
FINISHED CENTER STAR BLOCK SIZE: 8" × 8" ◆ FINISHED SMALL STAR BLOCK SIZE: 4" × 4"

Designed by Kim Diehl. Pieced by Julia Wareing. Machine quilted by Lois Walker.

5. Draw a diagonal sewing line on the wrong side of each of the eight teal 4½" squares as previously instructed. Layer a prepared teal square onto one end of a gray star unit as shown. Stitch, press, and trim as before to form a teal star point. In the same manner, add a mirror-image teal star point to the remaining end of the unit. Repeat to piece a total of four gray side-star units measuring 4½" × 8½", including the seam allowances.

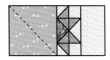 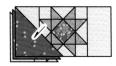

Make 4 gray side-star units,
4½" × 8½".

6. Lay out the four gray side-star units, the four turquoise small Star blocks from step 3, and the center Star block in three horizontal rows. Join the pieces in each row. Press. Join the rows. Press. The pieced quilt center should measure 16½" square, including the seam allowances.

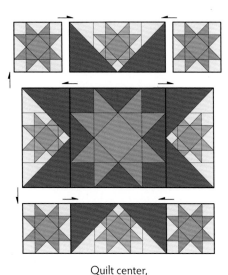

Quilt center,
16½" × 16½"

PIECING AND ADDING THE BORDER

1. Draw a diagonal sewing line on the wrong side of 16 gray 2½" squares and the 16 reserved teal 2½" squares as previously instructed.

2. Layer, stitch, press, and trim a prepared teal square onto the left end of an aqua 2½" × 4½" rectangle as previously instructed to form a teal triangle. In the same manner, use a prepared gray 2½" square to add a mirror-image triangle to the right end of the aqua rectangle. Repeat to piece eight flying-geese A units measuring 2½" × 4½", including the seam allowances.

Make 8 A units,
2½" × 4½".

3. Repeat step 2, reversing the placement of the gray and teal colors, to piece eight flying-geese B units measuring 2½" × 4½", including the seam allowances.

Make 8 B units,
2½" × 4½".

4. Lay out two flying-geese A units from step 2 and two flying-geese B units from step 3 in alternating positions. Join the units. Press. Repeat to piece a total of four border units measuring 2½" × 16½", including the seam allowances.

Make 4 border units,
2½" × 16½".

5. Using the quilt assembly diagram as a guide, join a border unit to the right and left sides of the quilt center. Press. Join a gray 2½" square to each end of

the remaining two border units. Press. Join these completed border units to the top and bottom edges of the quilt center. Press.

COMPLETING THE QUILT

Layer and baste the quilt top, batting, and backing. The featured quilt is machine quilted with straight echoed lines radiating out from the star points to the center squares; the on-point square in the center of the quilt is stitched with a small crosshatch. The cream background areas are filled with a small stipple design. The gray and teal portions of the flying-geese border are stitched with shallow repeating V shapes to resemble swags. Straight lines are stitched in the aqua border areas with Xs in the gray corner squares. Join the teal binding strips to make one length and use it to bind the quilt.

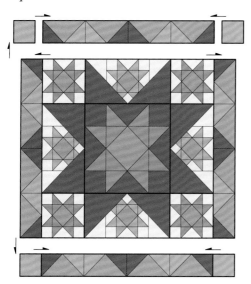

Quilt assembly

Making Waves

Triangle shapes can result in striking quilts and bring tons of layout options, but they're sometimes intimidating to sew—as a self-taught quilter, I know this firsthand! Through a little trial and error (OK, maybe a lot of error), I've learned to accurately stitch triangles, and I'm happy to share my best tips (see page 109) to help you achieve great results.

MATERIALS

Yardage is based on a 42" width of useable fabric after prewashing and removing selvages.

- 4 fat quarters (18" × 21") of assorted cream prints for large and small half-square-triangle units, flying-geese units, and center square-in-a-square unit
- 1 fat quarter of black print for large and small half-square-triangle units, flying-geese units, and binding
- 23 chubby sixteenths (9" × 10½") of assorted prints for large and small half-square-triangle units, flying-geese units, and center square-in-a-square unit
- 1 yard of fabric for backing
- 31" × 31" square of batting

CUTTING

Cut all pieces across the width of the fabric in the order given unless otherwise noted. The cutting instructions below will yield a handful of extra pieces in each given size to provide you with added choices as you stitch the patchwork.

From *each* of the 4 assorted cream prints, cut:
5 squares, 3⅞" × 3⅞" (combined total of 20); cut each square in half diagonally *once* to yield 2 large triangles (combined total of 40)
21 squares, 1⅞" × 1⅞" (combined total of 84); cut each square in half diagonally *once* to yield 2 small triangles (combined total of 168)
24 squares, 1½" × 1½" (combined total of 96)

From the black print, cut:
5 binding strips, 2½" × 21" (for my chubby-binding method provided on page 126, reduce the strip width to 2")
Reserve the remainder of the black print.

From *each* of the 23 assorted prints and the remainder of the black print, cut:
1 square, 3⅞" × 3⅞" (combined total of 24); cut each square in half diagonally *once* to yield 2 large triangles (combined total of 48)
4 squares, 1⅞" × 1⅞" (combined total of 96); cut each square in half diagonally *once* to yield 2 small triangles (combined total of 192)
2 rectangles, 1½" × 2½" (combined total of 48)

From the scraps of one assorted print, cut:
1 square, 2½" × 2½" (for the center square-in-a-square unit)

Piecing the Large and Small Half-Square-Triangle Units

Sew all pieces with right sides together using a ¼" seam allowance unless otherwise noted. Press the seam allowances as indicated by the arrows or as otherwise specified.

1. Join a cream and a print large triangle along the diagonal edges. Press. Trim away the dog-ear points. Repeat to piece a total of 36 large half-square-triangle units measuring 3½" square, including the seam allowances.

Make 36 large units,
3½" × 3½".

2. Using the cream and assorted print small triangles, repeat step 1 to make a total of 160 small half-square-triangle units measuring 1½" square, including the seam allowances.

Make 160 small units,
1½" × 1½".

Piecing the Flying-Geese Units

1. Use a pencil and an acrylic ruler to draw a diagonal sewing line from corner to corner on the wrong side of each cream print 1½" square.

2. Choosing the cream prints randomly, select two prepared cream 1½" squares and one assorted print 1½" × 2½" rectangle. Layer a prepared cream square onto one end of the rectangle. Stitch the pair together along the drawn diagonal line. Fold the resulting inner triangle open, aligning the corner with the corner of the rectangle; press. Trim away the layers beneath the top triangle, leaving a ¼" seam allowance. In the same manner, layer, stitch, press, and trim a second prepared 1½" square to the remaining end of the rectangle, to form a mirror-image triangle. Repeat to piece a total of 44 flying-geese units measuring 1½" × 2½", including the seam allowances. Reserve the remaining prepared cream squares.

Make 44 units,
1½" × 2½".

Piecing the Square-in-a-Square Unit

Layer two reserved prepared cream 1½" squares onto opposite diagonal corners of the print 2½" square. Stitch, press, and trim as previously instructed. Repeat with the remaining corners of the square to complete a square-in-a-square unit, measuring 2½" square, including the seam allowances.

Make 1 unit,
2½" × 2½".

Piecing the Sawtooth Sashing Strips

1. Lay out three small half-square-triangle units in one vertical row as shown. Join the units. Press. Repeat to piece a total of 12 short sawtooth sashing strips measuring 1½" × 3½", including the seam allowances. In the same manner, piece 12 short mirror-image sawtooth sashing strips.

Make 12 of each unit,
1½" × 3½".

2. Lay out 11 small half-square-triangle units in one horizontal row as shown. Join the units. Press. Repeat to piece a total of four long sawtooth sashing strips measuring 1½" × 11½", including the seam allowances. In the same manner, make four long mirror-image sawtooth sashing strips.

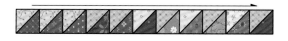

Make 4 of each unit,
1½" × 11½".

FINISHED QUILT SIZE: 24½" × 24½"

Designed and pieced by Kim Diehl. Machine quilted by Connie Tabor.

PIECING THE FLYING-GEESE SASHING STRIPS

Lay out 11 flying-geese units in one row as shown. Join the units. Press. Repeat to piece a total of four flying-geese sashing strips measuring 2½" × 11½", including the seam allowances.

Make 4 units, 2½" × 11½".

PIECING THE QUILT TOP

1. Lay out nine large half-square-triangle units, six short sawtooth sashing strips, and two long sawtooth sashing strips in three horizontal rows as shown. Join the large half-square-triangle units and short sawtooth sashing strips in each row. Press. Join the rows. Press. Repeat for a total of two pieced patchwork quadrants measuring 11½"' square, including the seam allowances. In the same manner, make two mirror-image pieced patchwork quadrants.

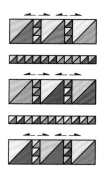
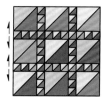

Make 2 quadrants, 11½" × 11½".

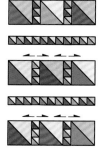
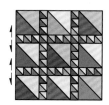

Make 2 mirror-image quadrants, 11½" × 11½".

2. Referring to the illustration, lay out the two patchwork quadrants, the two mirror-image patchwork quadrants, four flying-geese sashing strips, and the square-in-a-square unit in three horizontal rows. Join the pieces in each row. Press. Join the rows. Press. The finished quilt top should measure 24½" square, including seam allowances.

Quilt assembly

COMPLETING THE QUILT

Layer the quilt top, batting, and backing. Quilt the layers. The featured project is machine quilted with an allover pattern of intermingled feathers, swirled lines, and strings of pearls. Join the black binding strips to make one length and use it to bind the quilt.

October Sunset

Treat yourself to some relaxing handwork as you stitch a bitty wooly bird and sprays of berries, nestled into a branch of burnished autumn leaves. Then, change things up, add a frame of simple patchwork, and go for the dramatic finish with big-stitch hand quilting—this sweet project brings a myriad of techniques to the table!

MATERIALS

Yardage for cotton fabrics is based on a 42" width of useable fabric after prewashing and removing selvages.

- 1 fat eighth (9" × 21") of muted red plaid or print for center-block background and sawtooth-border patchwork
- 1 rectangle, 3" × 5", of brown wool for oak-leaf appliqué
- 1 strip, ¼" × 7¼", of tan wool for branch appliqué
- Scraps of wool in shades of black, gray, gold, orange, green, and blue for remaining appliqués
- Assorted cotton print scraps, equivalent to approximately one fat eighth (9" × 21"), for checkerboard and sawtooth borders
- 1 fat eighth of black print for binding
- 1 fat quarter (18" × 21") of fabric for backing
- 12" × 15" rectangle of batting
- Scraps of paper-backed fusible web (If you've opted to use my wool-appliqué method provided on page 114, my preference is HeatnBond Lite.)
- Water-soluble fabric glue
- Water-soluble marker
- #12 variegated perle cotton for stitching the appliqués and big-stitch hand quilting (I used Valdani's Bronze, color P9, for the branch; Ebony Almond, color O501, for the remaining appliqués and big-stitch hand quilting; and Aged White Medium, color P3, for the embroidered stems.)
- Size 5 embroidery needle
- Supplies for your favorite wool-appliqué method

CUTTING THE COTTON FABRICS

Cut all pieces across the width of the fabric in the order given unless otherwise noted. You may wish to cut an extra handful of the 1½" squares for added choices as you stitch the patchwork. Please note that for a scrappier look, I used only 1 triangle cut from each of the 1⅞" squares called for below; if desired, you can cut half the number of squares specified and use both triangles cut from each.

From the red plaid or print, cut:
1 strip, 7" × 10½"; from this strip, cut:
    1 rectangle, 7" × 8"
    3 squares, 1⅞" × 1⅞"; cut each square in half diagonally *once* to yield 2 triangles (total of 6)
1 strip, 1⅞" × 10½"; crosscut into 5 squares, 1⅞" × 1⅞". Cut each square in half diagonally *once* to yield 2 triangles (total of 10; combined total of 16 with previously cut triangles).

From the assorted print scraps, cut:
30 squares, 1½" × 1½"
16 squares, 1⅞" × 1⅞"; cut each square in half diagonally *once* to yield two triangles (combined total of 32)

From the black print for binding, cut:
3 binding strips, 2½" × 21" (for my chubby-binding method on page 126, reduce the strip width to 2")

then trim away the excess portion of the patch that extends beyond the leaf edge. Once the patch has been trimmed, the paper backing on the leaf can be removed.

5. Using the appliqué placement illustration as a guide, lay out the appliqués and branch, saving the berries for last because they can be used to fill in large open areas or easily arranged to fit in smaller areas. When you're pleased with the arrangement, work from the bottom layer to the top to apply small dots of liquid fabric glue at approximately ¼" intervals along the branch and the fusible web that rims each shape. Reposition the appliqués onto the red background, tucking the end of the branch approximately ¼" under the oak leaf.

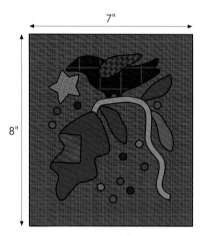

Appliqué placement

APPLIQUÉING THE CENTER BLOCK

1. Use a pencil to trace one each of the appliqué patterns (excluding the berries) provided on page 118 onto the paper side of the fusible web, leaving approximately ½" between each shape. Trace 12 berries, spacing them more closely together. Please note that no fusible web is needed for the branch.

2. Cut out the appliqués a scant ¼" *outside* the traced line of each shape. Next, excluding the berries, cut away the center of the fusible web inside each shape, approximately ¼" *inside* the traced line. (This technique is called "windowing," and will reduce bulk in larger shapes for more pliable appliqués.) Because of the small size of the berries, this windowing step isn't necessary.

3. Using the pictured quilt on page 115 as a guide for color choices, use a hot, dry iron to adhere the fusible-web shapes to the wool. Cut out the shapes exactly on the drawn lines. With the exception of the oak-leaf appliqué, peel away the paper backings.

4. For the oak leaf, while the paper backing is still in place, position the patch in a way that pleases you, heat set it from the back of the leaf with a hot, dry iron, and

✦ EXTRA SNIPPET ✦

Easy Paper Removal

Years of stitching wool appliqué has taught me that trying to separate the paper backing from the appliqués along the *outer* edges can be difficult, fraying both your nerves *and* the wool fabric. Instead, I've learned to use the tip of a straight pin or an embroidery needle to lift the paper edge from the *inside* of the appliqué, and then peel it away from the wool. Works like a charm!

October Sunset

FINISHED QUILT SIZE: 8½" × 11½"

Designed, appliquéd, pieced, and hand quilted in the big-stitch style by Kim Diehl.

6. Referring once again to the appliqué placement illustration on page 114, use a water-soluble marker to draw freeform stem lines from the branch to the berry clusters. This is your chance to add your own creative touch to the design, so don't worry about exactly duplicating the look of the featured quilt.

7. Referring to the stitch examples provided below, use a whip stitch (also called an overhand stitch) and the perle cotton to stitch the appliqués, a zigzag stitch (also called an arrowhead stitch) to secure the branch in place, a small-scale stem stitch for the stems, and a French knot to form the eye of the bird.

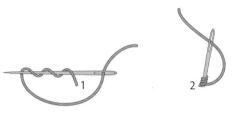

French knot

Stem stitch

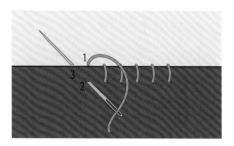

Whipstitch

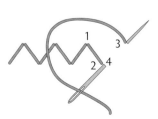

Zigzag stitch

8. Because the red background rectangle was cut slightly larger than needed to compensate for any possible shrinkage or fraying during the stitching process, now is the time to trim it to exactly the needed size. Use a rotary cutter and an acrylic ruler to trim the rectangle to 6½" × 7½", keeping the design centered.

PIECING AND ADDING THE CHECKERBOARD BORDER

1. Lay out seven assorted print 1½" squares end to end to form a short checkerboard row. Join the squares. Press. Repeat to piece two short checkerboard rows measuring 1½" × 7½", including the seam allowances. Join these rows to the right and left sides of the center block. Press the seam allowances away from the center block.

Make 2 short rows,
1½" × 7½".

2. Using eight assorted print 1½" squares for each row, repeat step 1 to piece two long checkerboard rows. Press the seam allowances in one direction. Join these pieced rows to the top and bottom edges of the center block. Press. The quilt top should now measure 8½" × 9½", including the seam allowances.

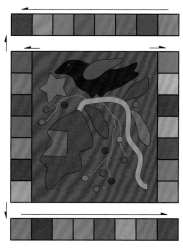

Quilt top,
8½" × 9½"

3. Layer a 1⅞" triangle cut from an assorted print onto a red 1⅞" triangle. Stitch the pair along the

diagonal edges. Press. Trim away the dog-ear points. Repeat to piece a total of 16 half-square-triangle units measuring 1½" square, including seam allowances.

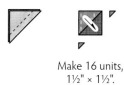

Make 16 units,
1½" × 1½".

4. Lay out eight half-square-triangle units to form a sawtooth row. Join the units. Press. Repeat to piece two sawtooth rows measuring 1½" × 8½", including the seam allowances. Referring to the illustration, join these pieced rows to the top and bottom edges of the quilt top. Press.

Adding the top and bottom borders

COMPLETING THE QUILT

Layer and baste the quilt top, batting, and backing. Quilt the layers. The featured quilt is hand quilted in the big-stitch style as described on page 126, with the appliqués outlined to emphasize their shapes and an approximate 1" crosshatch design used to fill in the background. The center block is stitched in the ditch (along the seamlines) and Xs are stitched onto the checkerboard squares. The sawtooth squares are stitched in the diagonal ditch, as well as ¼" out from each side of the diagonal seams. Join the black binding strips to make one length and use it to bind the quilt.

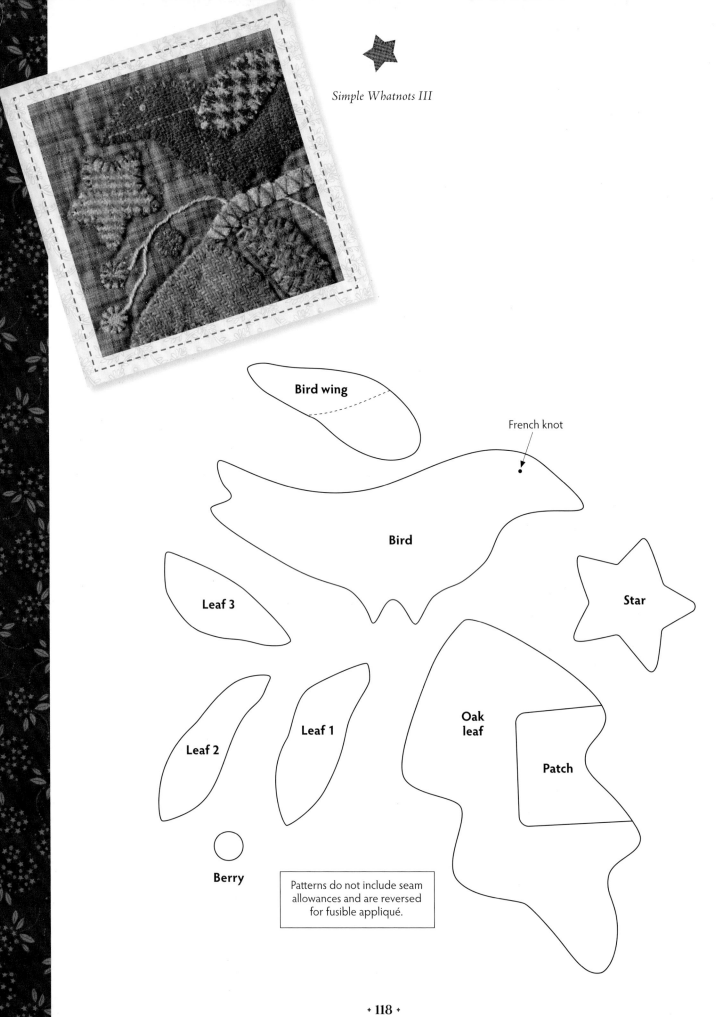

Simple Whatnots III

Bird wing

French knot

Bird

Star

Leaf 3

Leaf 1

Leaf 2

Oak leaf

Patch

Berry

Patterns do not include seam allowances and are reversed for fusible appliqué.

Kim's Quiltmaking Basics

The section that follows provides tons of how-to information to guide you through the quiltmaking steps in a simple and approachable way.

ROTARY CUTTING

Unless otherwise instructed, all pieces should be cut across the width of the fabric, from selvage to selvage. To streamline this step, I routinely fold my pressed fabric in half with the selvage edges together, and then align them with a marked line on the cutting mat. For the smaller-scale patchwork featured in this book, I often fold the fabric in half once more to achieve four layered pieces with each cut.

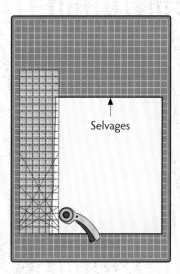

CUTTING BIAS STRIPS

1. After pressing the fabric to remove any wrinkles, lay it in a single layer on a large cutting mat. Fold one corner of the cloth back to form a two-layered triangle, aligning the straight edges of the fabric.

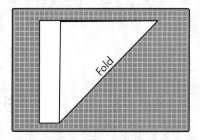

2. Rotate the layered piece of cloth to align the long diagonal fold with a marked line on the cutting mat (this will prevent a dogleg curve in the strips after they've been cut and unfolded).

3. Use a rotary cutter and an acrylic ruler to cut through the folded edge of cloth a few inches in from one pointed end. Work outward from this straight edge to cut strips in the width specified in the project directions.

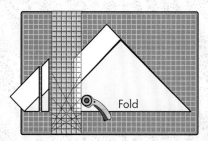

4. Square off the strip ends and trim them to the needed stem length, or join multiple squared-off lengths to form the specified length for vines or binding strips.

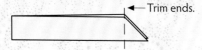

← Trim ends.

PINNING

I recommend pinning your patchwork at regular intervals, including all sewn seams. I routinely pin the bottom edge of each patchwork unit (where fishtailing can occur), as this enables me to lay my fingertip over the pinhead to guide the unit under the presser foot in a straight line.

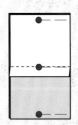

MACHINE PIECING

Unless otherwise instructed, join your fabrics with right sides together using a ¼" seam allowance. I prefer to shorten my sewing machine's stitch length from 2.2 to 1.8 for all patchwork projects to produce secure, less visible seams from edge to edge.

For projects with many units to be joined, chain piecing will increase your speed and save thread. Simply feed the pieces through the sewing machine one after the other without snipping the threads in between; once the stitching is complete, cut the threads between units to separate them.

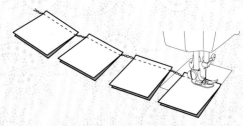

PRESSING SEAM ALLOWANCES

1. Place the patchwork unit on your ironing surface with the fabric you wish to press toward on top. Bring the iron down onto the seam to warm the cloth. While the cloth is still warm, fold the top layer of cloth back and run your fingernail along the line of stitching to open the layers all the way to the seam line. Press the opened layers with a hot iron. The seam allowances will now lie under the fabric that was originally positioned on top.

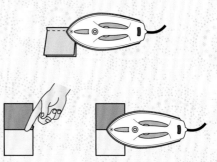

2. Once the block or patchwork is complete, lay it *wrong* side up on the ironing surface, apply a light mist of Best Press (or water), and use a hot iron to set the seams firmly in place. Pressing from the back will help ensure that the seams are resting flat and in the intended direction.

STITCH-AND-FOLD TRIANGLE UNITS

1. After cutting the pieces specified in the project instructions, use a pencil and an acrylic ruler to draw a diagonal sewing line from corner to corner on the wrong side of the square that will be used to stitch the triangle. Layer and stitch the patchwork, sewing the pair together along the drawn line.

2. Fold the resulting inner triangle open, aligning the corner with the corner of the square or rectangle beneath it to keep it square. Press. Trim away the layers beneath the top triangle, leaving ¼" seam allowances.

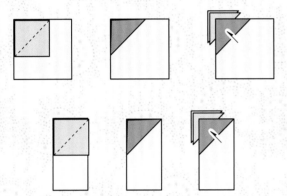

Traditionally, the excess layers beneath the top triangle are trimmed *before* the unit is pressed, but I've found that changing the order of the steps helps produce more accurate results and often eliminates the need to square up the finished unit.

INVISIBLE MACHINE APPLIQUÉ

In addition to standard quiltmaking supplies, you need the following items for my invisible machine-appliqué method:

- Sewing machine with an open-toe presser foot, featuring adjustable tension and the ability to produce a tiny zigzag stitch
- .004 monofilament thread in smoke and clear colors
- Awl or stiletto with a sharp point
- Bias bars in various widths
- Embroidery scissors with a fine, sharp point
- Freezer paper

- Lightweight iron or travel-size iron with a pointed pressing tip
- Fabric glue in both liquid and stick form, water-soluble (not permanent) and acid-free
- Pressing board with a firm surface
- Size 75/11 machine quilting or 60/8 universal sewing-machine needles
- Tweezers with rounded tips

Preparing Pattern-Tracing Templates

A tracing template is simply a tool that enables you to easily and consistently duplicate shapes when making multiple pattern pieces, eliminating the need to trace over the top of a pattern sheet numerous times. Remember, any time a pattern template is used, only one will be needed.

1. To prepare a tracing template, cut a single piece of freezer paper about twice as large as your shape. Use a pencil to trace the pattern onto the dull, nonwaxy side of the paper.

2. Fold the freezer paper in half, waxy sides together, and use a hot, dry iron to fuse the layers. From this fused piece, cut out the shape on the drawn lines to produce a sturdy template that can easily be traced around.

Preparing Freezer-Paper Pattern Pieces

Pattern pieces are the individual freezer-paper shapes used to prepare and stitch the appliqués from cloth. Always cut paper pattern pieces on the drawn lines, as the seam allowances will be added later when the appliqués are cut from fabric.

Use the prepared tracing template (or pattern sheet, if only a handful of pieces are needed) to trace the specified number of shapes onto the dull, nonwaxy side of a piece of freezer paper. Cut out the shapes on the drawn lines.

To easily make multiple pattern pieces, stack up to five additional layers of freezer paper underneath the top traced piece, all with the dull, nonwaxy paper sides up. Anchor the center of the shape with a pin to prevent shifting or use staples at regular intervals in the background around the shape. Cut out the pattern pieces on the drawn lines and discard the background areas.

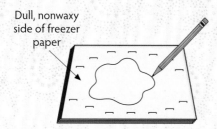

Dull, nonwaxy side of freezer paper

To prepare mirror-image pattern pieces, trace the pattern onto the dull, nonwaxy paper end of a strip of freezer paper, and then fold it accordion-style in widths to fit your shape. Anchor the layers and cut out the pieces as previously instructed. When the layers are separated, every other piece will be a mirror image.

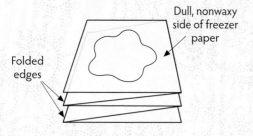

Dull, nonwaxy side of freezer paper

Folded edges

Preparing the Appliqués

1. Apply a small amount of fabric glue stick to the center of the dull, nonwaxy side of a freezer-paper pattern piece; affix the pattern piece to the wrong side of the fabric, shiny side up. Repeat with the remaining pattern pieces, leaving approximately ½" between each shape on the fabric for seam allowances.

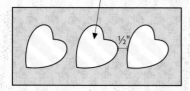

Wrong side of fabric, freezer paper waxy side up

½"

2. Using embroidery scissors, cut out each shape, adding an approximate ¼" seam allowance around the paper. Keep in mind that cutting the seam allowance in too scant a width will make it difficult to work with, while cutting too thick a width will add

bulk. As you practice the preparation steps and become comfortable with this technique, you'll find the width that works perfectly for you.

3. To make it easier to finish the appliqué edges, clip the seam allowance at any pronounced inner point or curve, stopping a couple threads away from the paper pattern piece. It isn't necessary to clip the seam allowances along any outer curves or points, only the inner portions.

Clip inner points, almost to paper edge.

Pressing Appliqués

Keep in mind as you work through the steps that follow that you'll want to work along the edge of the appliqué that's farthest away from you, rotating the appliqué toward the point of your iron as you work in one direction from start to finish. Always begin pressing along a straight edge or at a gentle curve, never at a point or a corner, because this will direct the seam allowance toward your "smart" hand (which is the hand that will hold the awl or stiletto) for later steps.

1. Use the pad of your finger to smooth the fabric seam allowance over onto the waxy side of the paper pattern piece, following with the point of a hot, dry iron to firmly press the cloth in place. (Please note that no glue is needed for this step, because there's enough stick on the waxy surface to hold the fabric in place on the paper pattern piece.) To avoid puckered appliqué edges, always draw the seam allowance slightly back toward the last section pressed, letting the point of the iron rest on each newly pressed area as you draw the next bit of cloth onto the pattern piece.

Direct seam allowance toward center of shape.

2. For sharp outer points, press the seam allowance so the folded edge extends beyond the paper pattern point. Fold over the seam allowance of the remaining side of the point and continue to complete the pressing. Apply a small amount of glue stick to the bottom of the folded flap of seam allowance at the point. Use the point of an awl or stiletto to drag the fabric in and away from the appliqué edge (not down from the point, as this will blunt it), and press with the point of the iron to fuse the layers in place. To hide the seam allowance at a narrow point, roll the seam allowance slightly under as you draw it in from the edge with the awl.

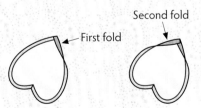

Second fold

First fold

To help achieve beautiful, sharp appliqué points, ensure that your pressed seam allowance hugs the paper edge on both sides of any given point as shown.

Wrong   Correct!

3. To prepare an inner point, stop pressing the seam allowance just shy of the center clipped section. Reaching under the appliqué at the clip, use the pad of your finger or the point of an awl to draw the clipped section of fabric snugly onto the paper, following immediately with the iron to fuse the cloth in place.

Making Bias-Tube Stems and Vines

To achieve finished stems and vines that can be curved flawlessly and don't require the seam allowances to be turned under, I use bias tubes. After cutting the strips specified in the project instructions (and referring to "Cutting Bias Strips" on page 119), prepare them as follows.

1. With wrong sides together (you'll want to be looking at the pretty, finished side of the print as you work through this step), fold the strip in half lengthwise. Use a scant ¼" seam allowance to stitch along the long raw edges to form a tube. For narrow stems, you'll likely need to trim the seam allowance to approximately ⅛" so that it will be hidden from the front of the finished stem.

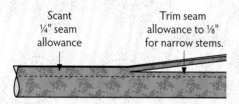

Scant ¼" seam allowance

Trim seam allowance to ⅛" for narrow stems.

2. Because of possible seam allowance differences, the best bias-bar width for each project can vary from the size specified. Ultimately, choose a bar that will fit comfortably into the sewn tube, positioning the seam allowance so it's resting flat to one side (not open), and centered from side to side. Press.

Bias bar

3. After removing the bias bar, place small dots of liquid fabric glue at approximately ½" intervals underneath the pressed seam allowance. Use a hot iron to heat set the glue and fuse the seam-allowance layers in place.

Basting Appliqués

Keep in mind as you lay out your design and baste the appliqués that there should be approximately ½" between the outermost appliqués and the raw edge of the background to preserve an intact margin of space around each piece.

1. Lay out the prepared appliqués on the background to establish the design, with any raw edges overlapped approximately ¼".

2. Remove all but the bottommost appliqués, and then baste them in place. My preferred method for this is glue basting because there are no pins to stitch around, the appliqués won't shift, and the background cloth won't shrink during the stitching process.

To glue baste, fold over one half of a positioned shape to expose the back; place small dots of liquid fabric glue along the fabric seam allowance (avoiding the paper pattern piece) at approximately ½" intervals. Unfold and reposition the glue-basted portion of the appliqué, repeat with the remaining half of the shape, and use a hot, dry iron from the back of the unit to heat set the glue and anchor the shape in place.

Preparing Your Sewing Machine

As you prepare your sewing machine, be sure to match the monofilament thread to your appliqué, choosing the smoke color for medium and dark prints and clear for bright colors and pastels.

1. Insert a size 75/11 machine-quilting needle (or a smaller 60/8 universal needle) in your sewing machine and thread it with monofilament.

2. Wind the bobbin with all-purpose neutral-colored thread. I suggest avoiding prewound bobbins because they can sometimes make it difficult to achieve perfectly balanced tension.

Note: If your machine's bobbin case features a "finger" with a special eye for use with embroidery techniques, feed your thread through this opening to help further regulate the tension.

3. Set your sewing machine to the zigzag stitch, adjust the width and length to achieve a tiny stitch as shown, and reduce the tension setting. For many sewing machines, a setting of 1 for the width, length, and tension produces the perfect stitch.

〰〰〰〰〰〰〰〰〰

Approximate stitch size

Stitching the Appliqués

The following steps will guide you through the stitching process. With a little practice, it's fun and easy!

1. Slide the basted appliqué under the presser foot from front to back to direct the threads behind the machine, positioning it to the left of the needle. Beginning at a straight or gently curved edge, anchor the monofilament tail with your finger as your machine takes two or three stitches. Release the thread and continue zigzag stitching around the shape, with the inner stitches landing just inside the appliqué and the outer stitches piercing the background immediately next to the appliqué. After a short distance, clip the monofilament thread tail.

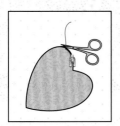

2. Continue stitching the appliqué at a slow to moderate speed, stopping and pivoting as often as needed to keep the edge of your shape feeding straight toward the needle.

+ If dots of bobbin thread appear along the top surface edge of your appliqué as you stitch, further reduce the tension setting until they disappear.

+ If the monofilament thread underneath your appliqué is visible from the back, or the stitches appear loose or loopy, gradually increase the tension setting as you stitch until they're secure.

3. For a secure inner appliqué point, stitch to the position where the inner stitch rests exactly inside the point of the shape and then stop. Pivot the piece and continue stitching.

Stop and pivot.   Continue stitching.

 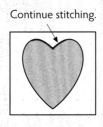

4. To secure an outer appliqué point, stitch to the position where the outer stitch lands exactly next to the appliqué point in the background and then stop. Pivot the piece and continue stitching.

Stop and pivot.   Continue stitching.

5. As you complete the stitching, overlap the starting point by approximately ¼" and end with a locking stitch. For machines without a locking stitch, extend your overlapped area to be approximately ½" long and your appliqué will remain secure.

String Appliqué

When two or more appliqués are positioned close together on the same layer, I recommend stitching your first appliqué as instructed in "Stitching the Appliqués," but instead of clipping the threads when you finish, lift the presser foot and slide the background to the next appliqué without lifting it from the sewing-machine surface. Lower the presser foot and resume stitching the next appliqué, remembering to end with a locking stitch or overlap your starting position by ¼" to ½". After the cluster of appliqués has been stitched, carefully clip the threads between each one.

Removing Paper Pattern Pieces

On the wrong side of the stitched appliqué, use embroidery scissors to carefully pinch and cut through the background fabric approximately ¼" inside the appliqué seam. Trim away the background, leaving a generous ¼" seam allowance. Grasp the appliqué edge between the thumb and finger of one hand and grab the seam allowances immediately opposite with the other hand. Give a gentle but firm tug to free the paper edge. Next, use your fingertip to loosen the glue anchoring the pattern piece to the fabric; peel away the paper. Any paper scraps that remain in the appliqué corners can be pulled out with a pair of tweezers.

Finishing Techniques

The guidelines that follow provide a variety of options for finishing and personalizing the look of your quilt.

Batting

For quilt tops using prewashed fabrics, I suggest using polyester batting or a cotton/polyester blend to ensure minimal shrinkage if your quilt is laundered. For quilt tops stitched from fabrics that weren't prewashed, I recommend choosing cotton batting, particularly if you love the slightly puckered look of vintage quilts.

Backing

I cut and piece my quilt backings to be approximately 3" larger than my quilt on each side. To prevent shadowing, it's generally best to use fabrics in colors similar to those in your quilt top.

Basting

For the smaller-sized projects featured in this book, I love the convenience of sandwiching the layers with basting spray, following the manufacturer's instructions.

Marking Quilting Designs

Masking tape or blue painter's tape in various widths makes an ideal guide for stitching straight lines. If you choose this method, keep in mind that all pieces of tape should be removed from the quilt top at the end of each day to prevent a sticky residue from forming on the cloth. More elaborate designs can be marked onto the top using a fine-tipped water-soluble marker before the layers are basted together.

Big-Stitch Hand Quilting

The big-stitch style of hand quilting is one of my favorite methods, because it's a quick and easy way to include hand stitching in my projects without a huge investment of time. For this style of quilting, I use a size 5 embroidery needle and #12 perle cotton to sew a running stitch (with each stitch approximately ⅛" to a scant ¼" long) through the quilt layers, ending my stitches as I would for traditional hand quilting.

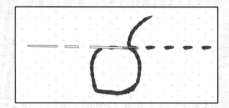

Machine Quilting

For in-depth machine-quilting instructions, please refer to 25 Days to Better Machine Quilting by Lori Kennedy. You'll see an edge-to-edge swirling pattern (think cinnamon rolls!) on many of my quilts when I want to add texture without introducing another design element. This pattern is shown below and is easy to stitch!

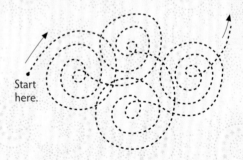

Start here.

Chubby Binding

Traditionally, a 2½"-wide French-fold binding is used to finish most quilts. For my quilts, I prefer a more unconventional chubby-binding method to produce a traditional look from the front of the quilt, with a wide strip of binding on the back.

To stitch chubby binding, you'll need 2"-wide strips and a bias-tape maker designed to produce 1"-wide double-fold tape.

1. Join the 2"-wide strips end to end without pressing the seams. Slide the pieced strip through the bias-tape maker, pressing the folds and seams with a hot, dry iron as they emerge.

2. Open the fold of the strip along the top edge only. Turn the beginning raw edge under ½" and finger-press the fold. Starting along one side of the quilt top (not at a corner), align the unfolded raw edge of the binding with the raw edge of the quilt. Use a ¼" seam allowance to stitch the binding along the raw edges. Stop sewing ¼" from the first corner and backstitch. Clip the thread and remove the quilt from under the presser foot.

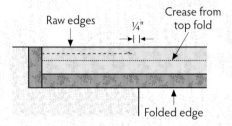

Raw edges   ¼"   Crease from top fold

Folded edge

3. Make a fold in the binding, then bring it up and back down onto itself to square the corner. Rotate the quilt 90° and reposition it under the presser foot. Resume sewing at the top edge of the quilt, continuing around the perimeter in this manner.

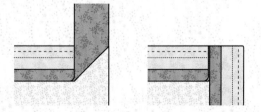

4. When you approach your starting point, cut the end to extend 1" beyond the folded edge and complete the stitching.

5. Bring the wide folded edge of the binding to the back and hand stitch it to the back of the quilt, enclosing the raw edges. Use a blind stitch and matching thread to hand sew the binding to the back. At each corner, fold the binding to form a miter and hand stitch it in place.

About the Author

After falling in love with a sampler quilt pattern in the late 1990s, Kim impulsively purchased it, taught herself the steps needed to make it, and then realized she was smitten with quiltmaking. As her newfound passion blossomed into a full-time career, Kim began publishing her original designs, traveling nationally to teach her approachable quiltmaking methods, and ultimately designing fabrics . . . a dream come true for a girl who once wondered if she had what it took to make a single quilt!

Modern time-saving techniques such as the easy invisible machine-appliqué method she's known for enable Kim to be prolific in her quiltmaking, and there's always something new in the works. Her very favorite quilts feature scrappy color schemes sewn from a mix of richly hued prints, and her designs often blend traditionally inspired patchwork with appliqué designs.

In addition to authoring numerous books, including her "Simple" series, Kim continues to design quilting fabric collections and Simple Whatnots Club projects in her signature scrap-basket style for Henry Glass & Co.

After retiring from an extensive travel and teaching schedule in 2015, Kim now spends her days at home doing what she loves most—designing quilts and fabrics, baking, stitching, gardening, and being a nana to her grandies.